WHITLEY BAY
PAST AND PRESENT

WHITLEY BAY
PAST AND PRESENT

JOHN ALEXANDER

First published in Great Britain in 2007 by
The Breedon Books Publishing Company Limited
Breedon House, 3 The Parker Centre, Derby, DE21 4SZ.

This paperback edition published in Great Britain in 2014 by DB Publishing, an
imprint of JMD Media Ltd

ISBN 978-1-78091-445-9

Printed and bound in the UK by Copytech (UK) Ltd Peterborough

CONTENTS

ACKNOWLEDGMENTS

Thanks go for the help and assistance in the preparation of this book to Eva, Jeffrey, Stephen and Rosie Alexander; Steve Caron and www.pictureclub.co.uk.

The book is also dedicated to the memory of my late fater, John Angus Alexander.

INTRODUCTION

This is my second book on Whitley Bay. The first was published in the year 2000. It had rave reviews and copies flew off the shelves. But it was not reprinted, despite the book shifting over 1,000 copies in the space of a month. A fine effort for a local book, by anyone's standards.

This book includes some pictures from the first work because there were literally hundreds of people left empty-handed wanting that book. But there are also well over 300 new fresh ones.

I am sure, like me, you will not only enjoy the photographs, but also the advertisements in this book. I find old adverts fascinating and no doubt you will too. The essesence of a good advert is to catch the eye of the reader and along with that they are also 'of their time' and this fact is demonstrated in the material included. Some adverts show a time of innocence, for instance, when the word 'gay' once meant happy.

My one regret is that I wish I had more images from the 1960s and 1970s in the book. These are quite rare, despite that period in time not being that long ago. I suppose the cost of processing photography was expensive back then. But now, because of the invention of high-quality digital cameras, there has been a resurgence in taking pictures – and that can only be a good thing for the future, as long as those images are kept and not erased from computers' hard drives!

You may find the end chapter lacking somewhat in 'old' photographs. This is done deliberately because I wanted to demonstrate how time flies fast and how swift changes can occur to a single town such as Whitley Bay. I call Chapter Five my 'now to become then' bit.

A few years back I was compiling a book about Newcastle for another publisher. I proposed an end chapter similar to the last in this book consisting of mainly photographs taken over the last five years to the present day. The editor said 'no, it's an old picture book'. I then took him to one side and said, 'It won't always be the year 2000' (the date of the publication).

And with that, he got the point. The book was published with that chapter included. It later went on to win an award and was chosen as one of only two books out of 100 republished by Marks and Spencer, the point being that even present day pictures become old and more relevant as time passes.

Another reason why this second book came about was because major changes have also occurred to the town since 2000, namely the new shopping mall in Park Avenue. Also, in February 2007, Whitley Bay learned that it had the go-ahead for the regeneration of the Spanish City, Library, Playhouse and surrounding areas.

Which leaves me to say – enjoy the book!

John Alexander, February 2007.

CHAPTER ONE

Around the Town

Whitley Road, *c.*1911. The familiar shops and tea houses which lined both sides of the street 100 years ago are long gone, although the road still remains. There are a few existing today in 2007 but a lot of the buildings are in a poor condition, with many shops closed and boarded up. The 'joke' at one time doing the rounds was that Whitley Bay was full of charity shops. But even they are now closing down.

These are some of the young apprentices who worked on Beaumont Park during the early 1970s. They were trained in Ashington, then moved to Whitley Bay to build the new housing estate. Many of the lads lived locally, so did not have far to travel to work each day. Their trades varied from bricklayers to painters and decorators.

This summer scene from the early 1930s was taken on Whitley Road, right outside what is now The Bedroom Pub – formerly known as The Vic. The mother's name is unknown, but the baby in the pram, if he/she were still alive, would be well into their mid-70s now.

View of the old pre-Metro Whitley Bay Railway station pictured around 1905. Unlike Tynemouth Station, which was graced with more ornate design and space, Whitley Bay station still managed to cater for the massive amount of passengers coming to and from the resort.

The hustle and bustle of Station Road, c.1912. Trade was very healthy for the stores that lined the road, because custom came both from local residents and holidaymakers arriving from the train to the seaside resort. The one thing lacking here compared to today, apart from heavy trading, are cars!

The Victoria Hotel. This grainy old picture was taken around 1900. It looks a fine building where the financially well-off people used to stay. It has stood well over 100 years, but whether it can avoid the bulldozer in the future is anyone's guess. Then the establishment had class – now it's predominately a drinking den and would-be nightclub area on Friday and Saturday nights.

An interesting view again outside The Vic, this time taken looking up to St Paul's Church. The photographer was standing where the current zebra crossing is. The tranquillity compared to today's fast-paced lifestyle is an intriguing comparison. And once again, glory glory – NO CARS or pollution.

A sad sight, and an eyesore if ever there was one. As the seaside resort's prosperity and popularity declined, derelict and boarded-up buildings became commonplace. This is former council offices, now happily flattened. A grass verge is better than looking at that monster!

Outside St Paul's Church on the corner of Marden Road, where the traffic lights are. In 1999 a derelict computer shop was where the entrance to the shopping mall now is. As you can see, the former owner has left the satellite dish up. It's a wonder it was not stolen as it remained up there unused for well over a year. The shop was then demolished to make way for the new shopping mall.

In 1978 the late actor Jimmy Jewel made a television series called *Funny Man*. The outside of The Allesta Ballroom in the Esplanade was changed into 'The Pavilion Theatre'. The tarmac road was also temporarily covered with TV effect rubber cobblestones. All this was necessary as the series was set in the 1930s and theatre's surroundings had to fit in with the times. The cobblestones are not seen here, because they would be out of camera shot anyway.

A Sunday morning in Whitley Road, 1977. The entrance to The Vic is to the right, where the parked car is. Little has changed in 30 years.

A familiar view looking down Marden Road, *c.*1900. St Paul's Church's spear is clearly visible. Ahead is the Rockcliff Motor Garage.

The 'New' Coliseum building in Whitley Road, summer 1979. It has housed everything from a cinema to a bingo hall. But will its place at the centre of Whitley Bay survive the demolition plans often drawn up by the council? Who knows. Some argue that if and when this area is flattened, it will return Whitley Bay back to its little village status. A controversial view, but one that is aired quite frequently in many quarters.

On the corner of Marden Road with the Co-op Building to your right, *c.*1900. Eagle-eyed readers will probably see thirsty customers drinking outside The Ship Pub, in the centre of the picture.

On the corner of Clarence Crescent and Station Road, outside the entrance to Whitley Bay Metro Station, *c.*1989. This old telephone/post office kiosk survived BT's introduction of the familiar modern box we see on our streets today, although they are quickly declining due to the increased use of mobile telephones. Now apparently regarded as a Grade II listed building, the cast-iron kiosk Number 4 was introduced in 1928 but had a short life. Fewer than 50 were installed when word got round that they were proving unpopular with customers. Not only did the postage stamp machine outside cause a racket which disturbed people making calls inside the box, but the stamps themselves became damp in cold weather and would occasionally cause blockages. The majority of the boxes were withdrawn in 1935, but this one was forgotten about.

Updated for its time, and with a new paint job, the outside of the telephone kiosk retains the appearance and feel of the 1930s, but inside bears little similarity to its original condition. The most notable difference is the modern telephone handset. Maybe one day as mobile telephone communications takeover, the box can be refitted with its original telephone, purely to add finishing touches to what will be, in effect, a display antique!

A quaint view of the bottom of Victoria Avenue, looking out toward the promenade. And two children have spotted the cameraman. This postcard dates from about 1910.

Defying the developers, June 1984. So far this beautiful, century-old Presbyterian church in the Esplanade has escaped plans to knock it down. Yet it seems nothing is entirely sacred, as a few other churches both in Whitley Bay and Cullercoats have ended up as rubble. Keep your fingers crossed.

Whitley Bay Railway Station in 1972. Not much has changed since then, all except it's now Metro operated and the old ticket boxes, to the right of the picture, are now a thing of the past. And who can forget the Beachnut chewing gum box fitted close to the newsagent's kiosk.

The majority of postcards centre on landmarks, such as the lighthouse and coast. This one of the railway station came in both black and white and a hand-coloured version. Note the absence of cars – not yet commonplace! Today in 2007 the cars are packed round here, and it's almost impossible to get a clear view of the station in all its glory.

Can you guess which side this train is coming from, Cullercoats or Monkseaton? The photograph is dated sometime around 1904, and belonged to the north-eastern Railway Collection. This particular image has been copied numerous times for postcards, but this one is the original.

A public toilet wall flattened by the violence of the waves, rather than vandals. This outside toilet at the bottom of Victoria Park was unkempt and smelly and eventually demolished due to hygiene complaints.

Now commonly known as The Fire Station pub, this is the real fire station, at the back, on York Road, around two years after it was closed down. It quickly fell into disrepair. The picture was taken in 2000.

Whitley Road on a Sunday morning in the 1980s. Peace and quiet – almost a ghost town! But not quite, back then the town woke up around 12 noon.

The long-forgotten Priory Theatre on Park Avenue, pictured here in the late 1970s. Popular local celebrity Mike Neville MBE once performed there in the 1950s. The former *Look North* and *Tyne Tees* newsreader was 16 years old and appeared in the play *The Man Who Came To Dinner*. He wanted to be an actor then but the 'bright lights' of the television news studio were where he ended up! As Mike recalls with immense fondness, and a lot of people agree with him, 'it's a pity we've lost the Priory'.

Looking in need of a makeover, The Allesta Ballroom, pictured here in 1969, was a cinema and many other things over the years. It was neither one thing or the other. It has looked good and bad from the outside over previous decades but now it's dubious as to whether it will still be around in 10 years time. A large old building like this needs love, care and constant attention – something it has been lacking in for many decades.

Whitley Bay's famous clock on the seafront is highly unreliable. Sometimes it works, then it does not. Its inability to maintain the correct time takes second place to the fact that it's still a worthy landmark, despite suffering from the occasional tasteless paint job. This one isn't too bad; its black and white strips were in celebration of Newcastle United Football Team.

The swivelling holiday chalets on Whitley Bay's Lower Promenade met their fate with the bulldozer in 1990. The chalets were in fairly-reasonable condition, which sparked minor opposition to the demolition, although it went ahead anyway. This picture, taken in 1987, fails to show that the chalets were painted in all the primary colours. And many people agree that it's so sad that they are no longer there.

The now long-gone Christian Science Church on Park View, opposite the library, proves one thing. Nothing stands in the way of what is considered progress, in this case luxury flats.

Whitley Bay Railway Station *c.*1918. These well wrapped-up commuters look like they are heading to work on a cold winter's day.

The line of lamps along Whitley Bay Seafront in the mid-1980s illuminate the road on bleak, dark nights, and also add a romantic feel to the surroundings on summer evenings.

It's the early 1990s and North Tyneside Council's crazy idea to make a pedestrian walkway out of a very busy Whitley Road caused laughter as well as mass anger. York Road, the narrow street behind The Vic, was used to divert the traffic causing chaos, with heavy goods vehicles, double-decker buses and other vehicles squeezing along the road. It did not take long for the system to be dumped, but not before costing council tax payers thousands and thousands of pounds of unnecessary expense and waste. Looking at the insanity of this picture, it's amazing and quite frightening how such a barmy idea ever got off the ground. Apart from looking ridiculous, what purpose did it serve?

The Ship Pub in the mid-1980s, quiet on a lazy Sunday morning. Believe it or not, at one time this watering hole used to close doors at 3pm, long before controversial extended opening hours got the go ahead.

Whitley Bay Police Station in Laburnum Avenue endeavours to keep criminals at 'bay' in the seaside town. No pun intended.

Arcadia in Whitley Road some 100 years ago. A tram travels toward the route to Cullercoats. The clarity of this postcard is harmed by a rather crude attempt to colour it in, leaving it effectively resembling a blurred watercolour.

Park Avenue, looking toward the Spanish City, *c*.1910. In the distance a large big wheel can be seen at the funfair area. And note the man or woman wearing that strange looking 'Scrooge' garb, to the right of the photograph.

Whitley Road, looking down to the left, South Parade. And in full view The Exchange Buildings; 100 years ago it was a valued mall, full of shops selling such diverse things from children's toys and ladies' clothes to electrician's wares and repairs, etc. Sadly, the large ornate three-piece lamp no longer exists.

Anyone for tennis? Friends make the most of their holiday at the courts in Victoria Park during the mid-1920s. It was not seen as 'quite decent' for young ladies to bare their legs, so the girls in this picture heed the fashions of the day by wearing thick, woollen socks, covered by equally chunky dark skirts. Not very comfortable to say the least, considering what must have been a sweltering heat. And cast an eye on those cumbersome wooden rackets.

A dark, faded postcard view of the Presbyterian Church in the Esplanade in 1903.

No doubt you will scratch your head and wonder where this is. Alas, it longer exists. The Povesi's Café and Restaurant occupied land on the Whitley Bay Front, not far from where the Leisure Pool stands now. Judging from the outside, the inside must have been just as wonderful.

Just how clothing can define a decade, the movie showing at the Coliseum pinpoints the year of this pretty postcard of Whitley Road. *Sea Devils* was made in 1953 and starred Rock Hudson and Yvonne De Carlo.

Not many postcard makers choose streets as their subject, opting first for places of interest. However, this photograph of Cambridge Avenue is a fine example of Whitley Bay in the early 1930s.

The tatty small building on the right is the Old Smithy on Whitley Road, pictured over 100 years ago. It's in the vicinity of where Woolworths now stands. On close inspection it appears to be a time of elections. A small board tipped on its side on the right of the picture says 'Vote for Hilton.'

It's not clear whether this is a dark, gloomy day in Oxford Street long ago, or the result of a photograph affected poorly by passing of time.

A classic photograph of the top of Percy Road. To the right is the Station Hotel, looking toward and along Whitley Road to the town centre. The hustle and bustle of the time makes the image a classic example of what has now vanished into a bygone era.

A wet day sees a civic procession travelling along Whitley Road, on the junction of South Parade and Victoria Terrace. The occupants on the horse and cart bear the Belvedere hallmark. The date is unknown.

Standing where the entrance to the Co-op is close to Park View, on the right is the Fat Ox Hotel. On the left is where the light crossing is. The date is around 1904.

Monkseaton Railway Station 100 years ago appeared to have just one platform where you could keep dry from the rain. Many stations were built that way.

Whitley Park Hall, built in 1789. Several owners of the mansion enlarged it and T.W. Bulman, who bought it in 1869, re-routed the road away from the hall and enclosed the estate with trees, many of which remain on one side of Park Avenue. In 1897 the estate was taken over by the Whitley Park Hotel Company, the hotel was sold to the council in 1922, who used it as offices, and it was demolished in 1939, with the grounds cultivated into a public park. The lodge just outside the gates at the top of Park Avenue survived until the building of the new library in 1966.

The bottom of Marden Road in 1980. This was probably taken on a Sunday morning or maybe Christmas or New Year's Day, judging from the lack of activity.

Another view of Acadia, Whitley Road, *c*.1900. The services of the same colouring postcard techniques appear to have been applied here, too. A bit over generous with the colours, though.

A delightful drawing of some areas of Whitley Bay and Monkseaton. With the areas being close to each other the boundaries often get blurred. From left to right, top to bottom are: Marine Avenue, Holywell Avenue, Black Horse and Ship Inns and Coronation Row, Briar Dene Golf Course, The Fold in 1893, Monkseaton Village, Brewery and Monkseaton Arms and Blacksmith's shop in 1893.

A similar drawing depicting more places in Whitley Bay; the sands, town centre, promenade, Table Rocks, and St Mary's Island are featured.

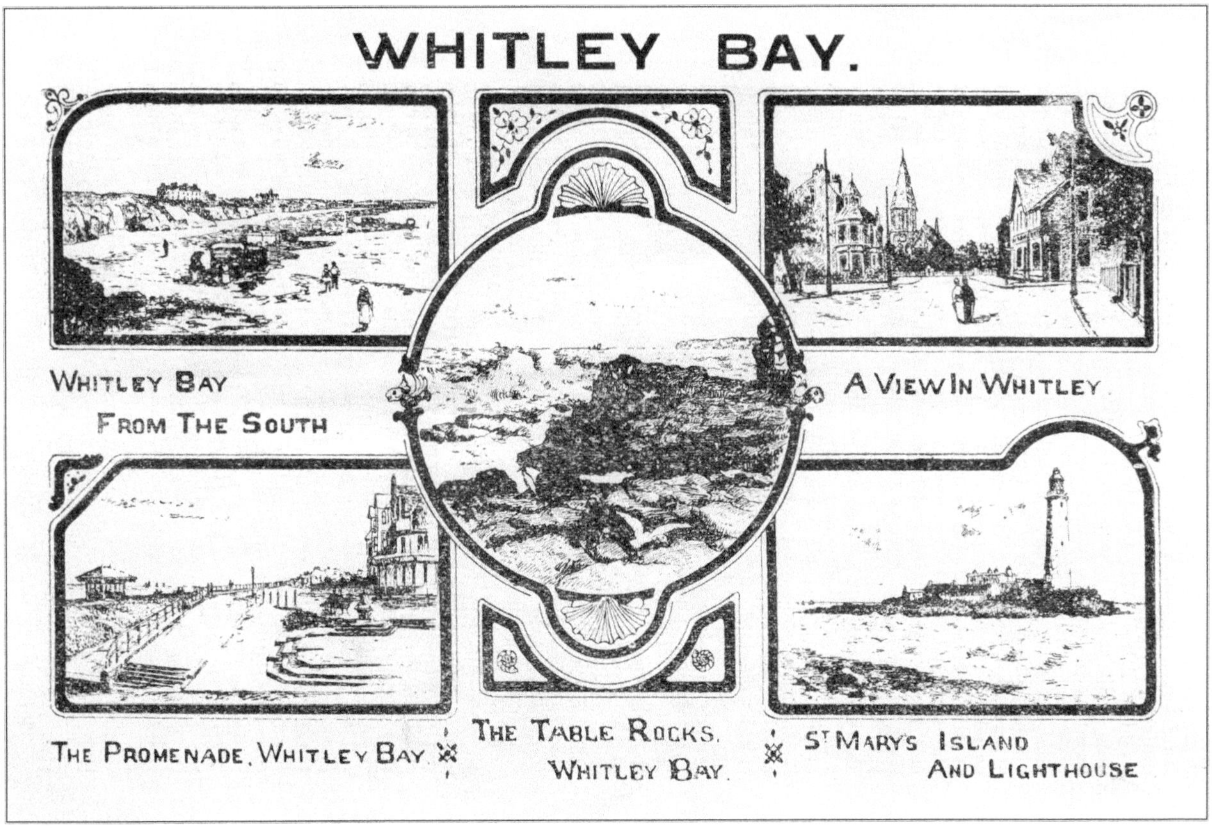

A hand-coloured picture postcard of St Paul's Church, taken around 1910.

Another view of St Paul's Church, from the same period and probably from the same postcard maker. But this time a side shot.

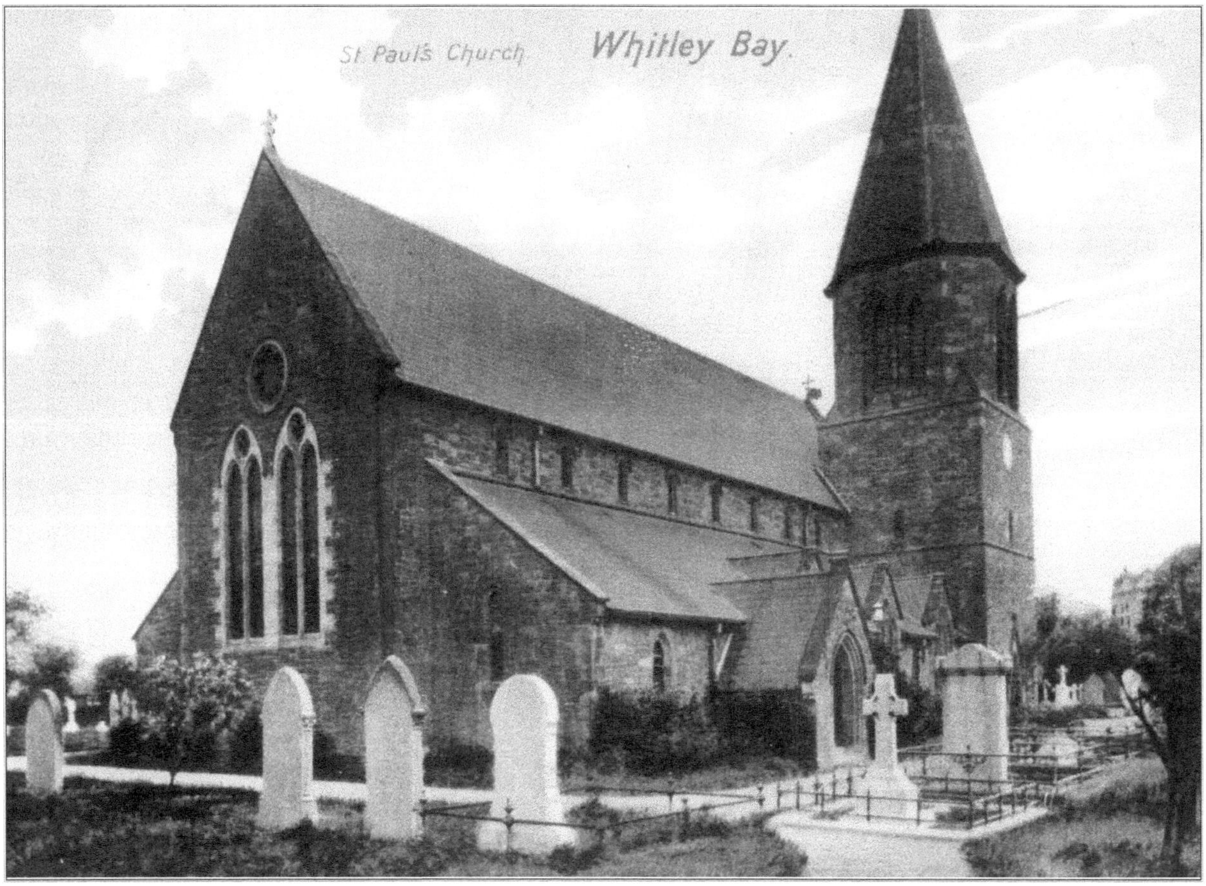

A summer scene in Whitley Bay Park, *c*.1950, in the vicinity of the grounds of where the current library is situated.

A curious and rare booklet cover explaining the merits of Whitley Bay's Sea Water Baths, date unknown. With Russian and electric hot and cold sea water at hand, it certainly would be a visit you would not forget. There was even an opportunity to enjoy regular picture concerts twice nightly!

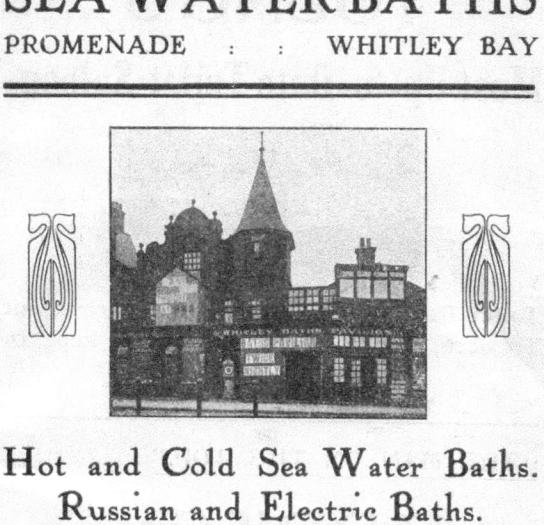

Count the line of cars pictured here! They are almost like an infinite mirror on mirror reflection. This plot at the bottom of Marden Road has occupied one business or other for many decades and still exists to this day, not as a garage but as a small recreational centre.

Girl on a bike in The Gardens, Monkseaton. This picture is 100 years old or more, but the identity of the girl remains a mystery. It was probably some close relative or friend of the photographer.

A mass of flowers and trees disguise the fact that there are three people in this picture of Whitley Bay Park, *c.*1950. An elderly couple in the centre and in the foreground a middle-aged man reading a newspaper.

You often find in old picture postcards, such as this one taken on Front Street, Monkseaton, people turning their heads to pose for the camera.

An intriguing old map of the coastline from Seaton Delaval to Cullercoats, mentioning such diverse places as the Convalescent Home in Whitley Bay to Cullercoats's Smuggler's Cave!

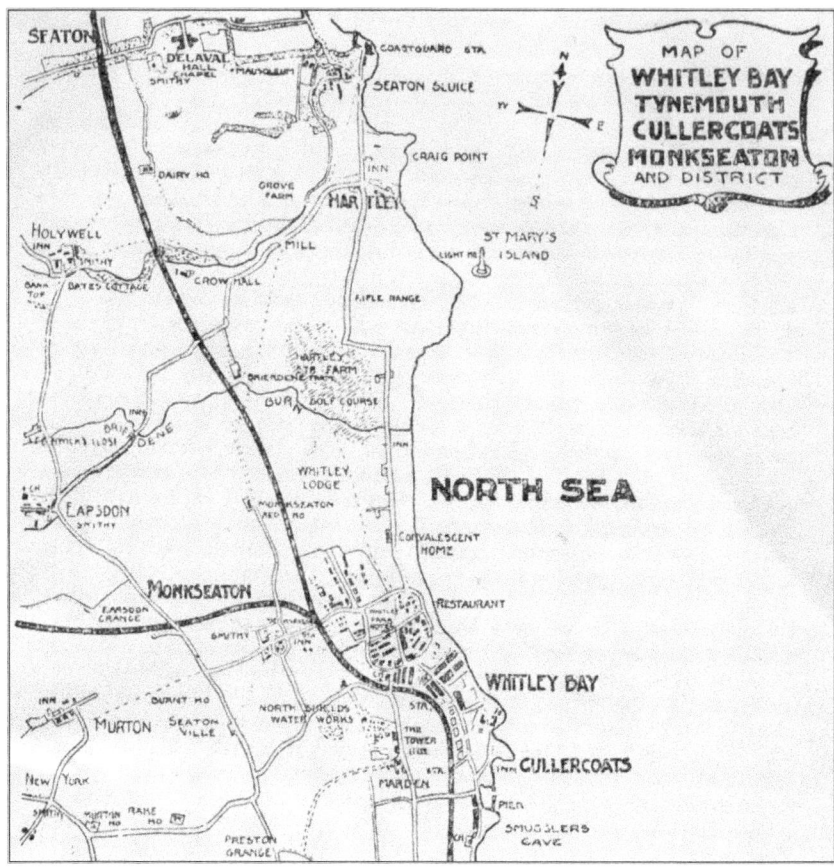

A gloomy day in the residential area of Eastbourne Gardens taken around 100 years ago.

Hardly Whitley Bay at The Bedroom on a Friday and Saturday night in summer months! The tranquillity of Whitley Bay was far more apparent at the start of the 20th century. Who reckons loud music and ecstatic merriment in those days would have sent the population of Whitley Bay insane?

The now demolished Post Office building in Park Avenue, seen here in the year 2000. Apparently it was Grade II listed, with many people at the time wrongly thinking it could be rescued from any proposed demolition plans and perhaps, instead, be converted into a cinema or entertainment complex, but it was regrettably not to be. Now all that remains of it are photographs. And rare ones at that!

The entrance to the bus station, with The Sands Club above. Sands saw its doors open in the mid-1960s after planning permission curiously got the go ahead, despite receiving some opposition from residents. It was renowned for its loud music and for breaking the hearts of many a young person who would travel far and wide from the likes of Gateshead and Newcastle to find love. That's the romantic way of putting it! Below The Sands was a bakers, a tobacco shop and a wool shop.

This area is where the shopping mall now stands. To the right of the picture are the back entrances to the likes of Finlays, Carters and Pound Stretcher. Steel's Nurseries also once occupied this spot a century ago and a second-hand car garage in the mid-1980s.

The year 2000 and behind the bus depot entrance. Buses lay in the garage overnight. One of the most commonly remembered buses to go through here was the 308 to Newcastle and Blyth.

Another view of the bus station. Commuters would wait here for their buses. Inside the building was the travel centre, where passes could be bought and bus holidays booked.

Park View in 1900. Right down the bottom and to the right is St Paul's Church.

Steel's Nurseries plot pictured here behind Park View 100 years ago.

Another image of Park View looking down to the direction of the Co-op – almost unrecognisable today.

The Sea Water Baths building was also material for postcard makers. Here's a picture taken during the height of its popularity. The postcard looks a bit grubby, though it was, after all, recovered from a bric-a-brac stall.

Whitley Bay Park sometime in the late 1940s. Not long after the war, rationing was still on. But these people appear to be coping well with the restrictions of the time. A calm walk in the park soothes the brain.

Yet another view of the Sea Water Baths. The colouring pens were out again in full force for this picture, which once again slightly spoils the clarity.

Sea Baths. : Whitley Bay.

It's a shame the photographer could not get closer to snap the mansion, which were turned into council offices. The park trees act as a distraction to the main object, a useful lesson in how not to take a picture!

The long-demolished Whitley Road Council Offices, next to the original building that was the Woolworths store, on Whitley Road.

Standing house-proud. Former occupants of one of the cosy terraced houses at the lower, Cullercoats end of Whitley Road pose for the camera during the mid-1930s. The railings were removed during World War Two – not to build planes and ships as people thought, but simply to make the public think that the general public were doing their bit for the war effort.

Park View in 1978. The year of *Grease* the film and the accession of the new Pope John Paul. The large store to the left of the picture is still very much active, not as Thoms as it was once known but as Poundstretcher.

R.A. Gofton Builders were so well established by the early 1950s, with nearly 60 years' experience of serving the community behind them, that they played a pivotal role in the major Whitley Bay and Monkseaton building programmes. Workers are seen here in the early 1930s. Today the business is still going strong, doing repairs and refitting picture and dado rails.

An open-top bus, or the Whitley Bay Police Force a very long time ago taking 'customers' to the cells! Due to its large size, such a vehicle would certainly turn the heads of the force today, as none of the occupants appear to be wearing the required seat belts.

Taken from a 1939 council tourist booklet explaining how people can find their way around Whitley Bay, this picture makes reference to the Public Offices.

A more detailed map of Whitley Bay, this time from 1938. Note the Rex Hotel is called the Waverley Hotel.

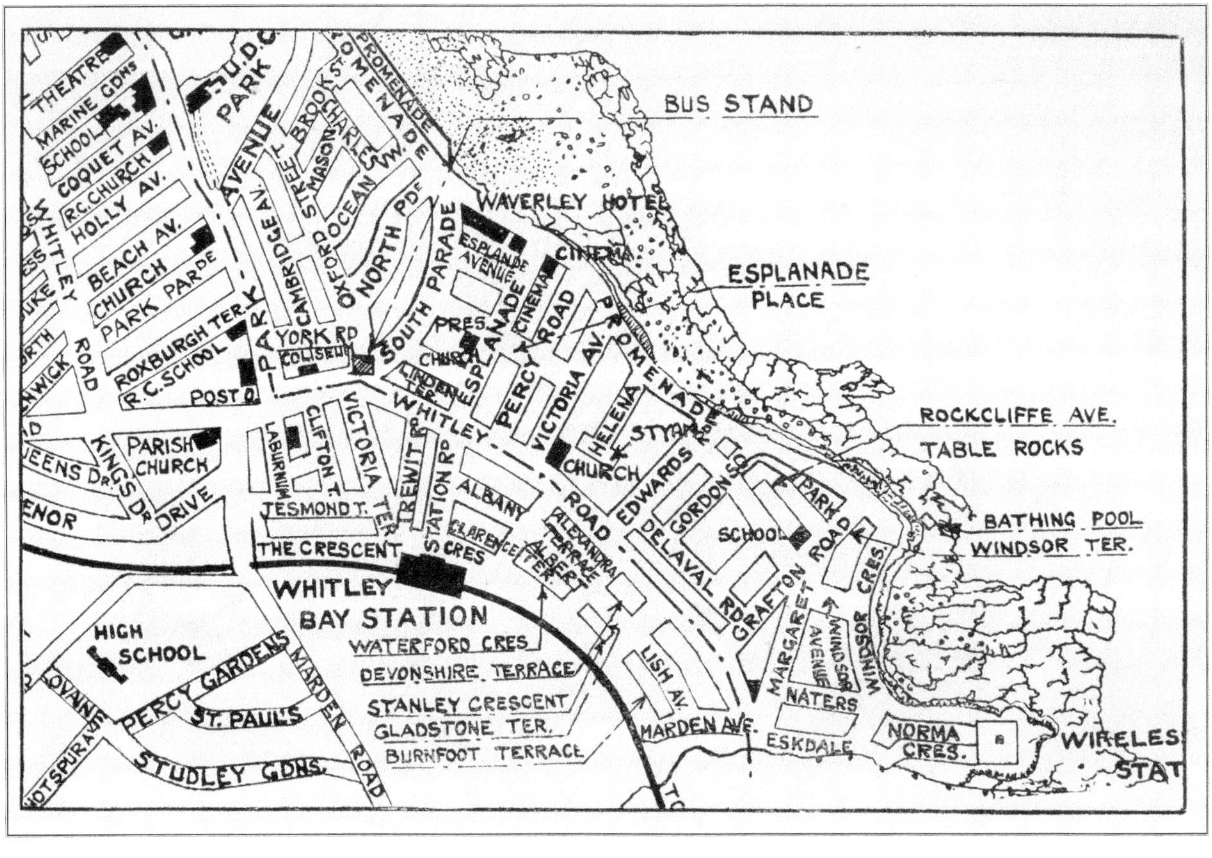

Just how not to expect South Parade back in 1910! Few licensed premises were allowed down this street, only guest houses with no desire to serve alcohol.

Monkseaton Arms in 1970, looking remarkably the same as it does today!

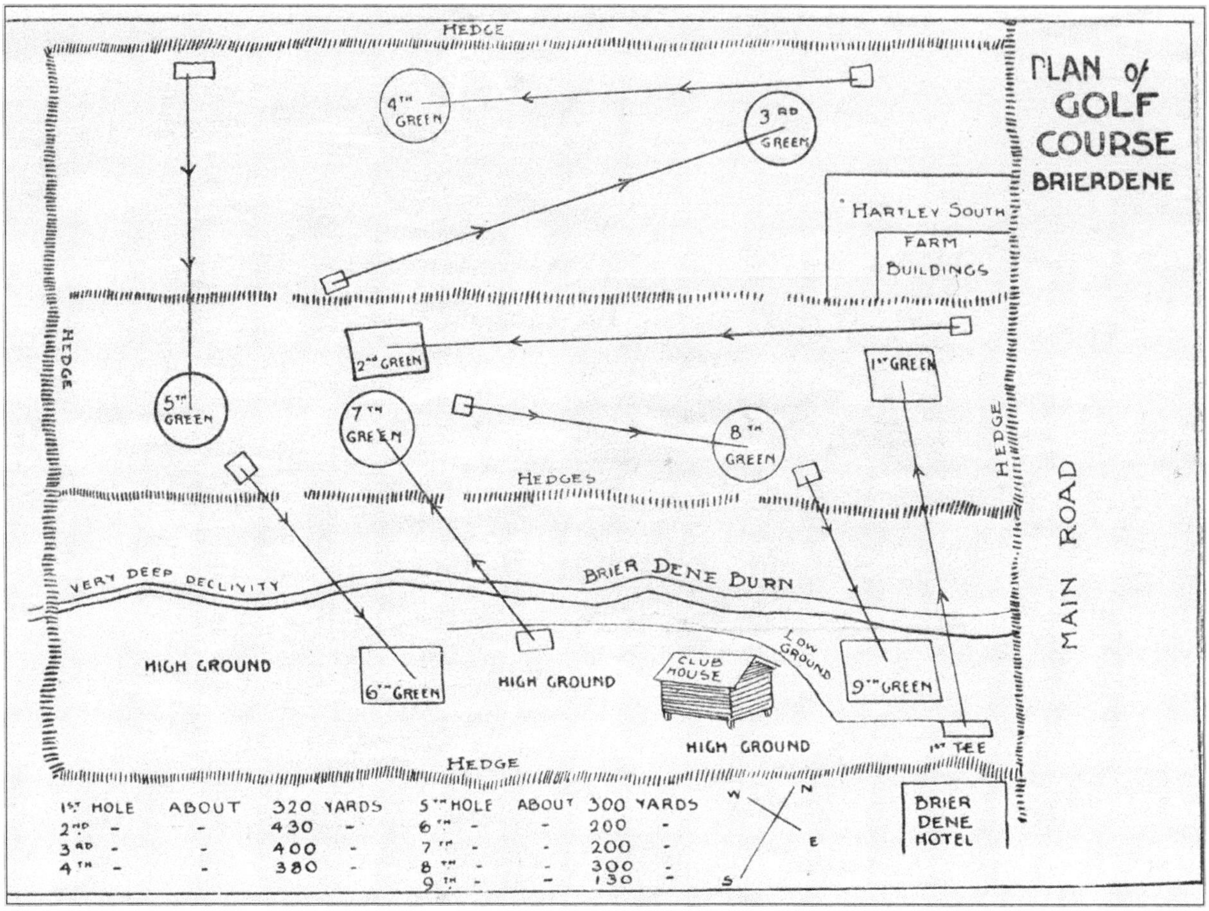
PLAN of GOLF COURSE BRIERDENE
HEDGE
4TH GREEN
3RD GREEN
HARTLEY SOUTH
FARM BUILDINGS
2ND GREEN
1ST GREEN
HEDGE
5TH GREEN
7TH GREEN
8TH GREEN
HEDGE
HEDGES
MAIN ROAD
VERY DEEP DECLIVITY
BRIER DENE BURN
LOW GROUND
HIGH GROUND
CLUB HOUSE
6TH GREEN
HIGH GROUND
9TH GREEN
HIGH GROUND
1ST TEE
HEDGE
BRIER DENE HOTEL
W N E S
1ST HOLE ABOUT 320 YARDS
2ND - - 430 -
3RD - - 400 -
4TH - - 380 -
5TH HOLE ABOUT 300 YARDS
6TH - - 200 -
7TH - - 200 -
8TH - - 300 -
9TH - - 130 -

This is a curious find. A 1938 plan for Whitley Bay Golf Course. But who drew it?

Who fancies a new car for just £168? Well, you would need a time machine first, because that was the price of a 1939 model at Fowler & Garland Ltd.

VAUXHALL Sales and Service
1939 Models In Stock. Prices From £168
We run our own fleet of VAUXHALLS let us service yours !
Phone 517
FOWLER & GARLAND LTD.
PARK GARAGE, (Adjoining Theatre) WHITLEY BAY
[See also page 16

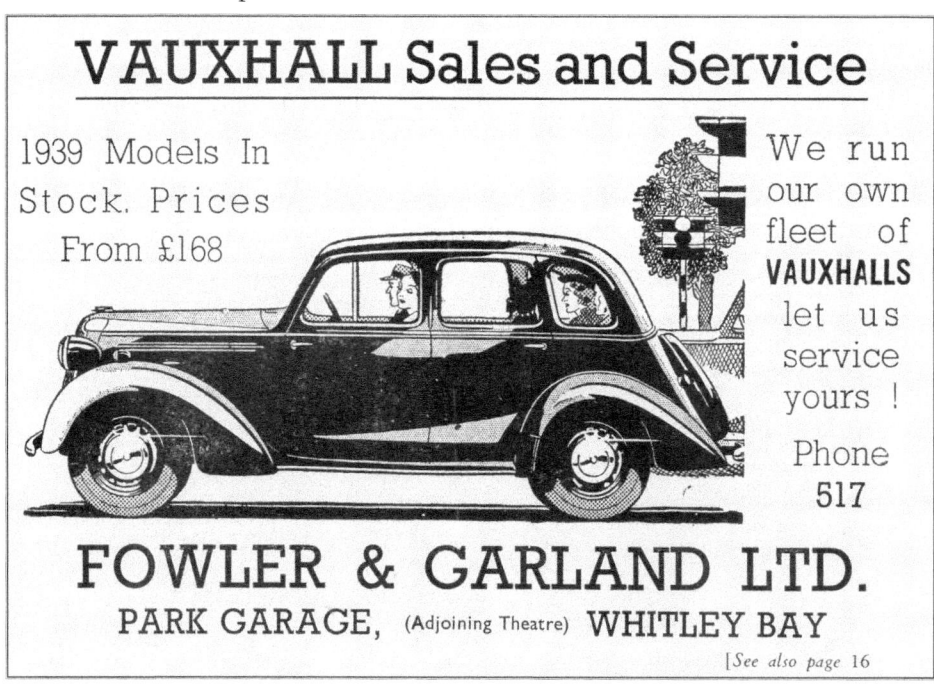

A dark night in Monkseaton in 1958. A man reads a newspaper at the bus stop, probably having just come from The Black Horse pub behind.

Looking over the wall at Monkseaton; to the right today is the Spar supermarket.

Some places never change. This area of Park Avenue, pictured above, is almost identical as it is today – remarkable considering this picture was taken around 80 years ago.

The Prudhoe Memorial Home on The Links, Whitley Bay, *c.*1926. A memorial to the fourth Duke of Northumberland, the home was opened on 14 September 1869. The local council bought the building and it was demolished in 1974 to make way for the Leisure Pool.

Whitley Road, Whitley Bay.

A quaint postcard from around 1910 looking down (right) Whitley Road and (left) South Parade.

The residential part of Whitley Bay in 1988. This is number 35 Briar Avenue, John Alexander's former dwelling!

Looking out from number 35 Briar Avenue to Davison Avenue on a snowy day in December 1992.

CHAPTER TWO

Tourists and Beach

A fantastic poster advertising the holiday resort of Whitley Bay. Originally in colour, the attraction looks more like the French Riviera than a north England beach!

The bottom of the avenue, at the heart of the tourist centre. This clear postcard from the early 1930s shows a hive of activity. But how many people in this day and age would leave two children in a small pram at the roadside – bottom right?

How times change. It's amazing to think just what drove hundreds of tourists to flock in their droves on what was termed Table Rocks, in Whitley Bay. It certainly would not happen today. But it must be remembered, life was much more simple then. It was not a materialistic world.

'Walking' cameraman Billy Hearn took many snaps of Whitley Bay, Cullercoats and Tynemouth seafronts. This one is believed to be from the late 1940s. The gentleman pictured went by the name of Jack, although his surname is a mystery. Perhaps the photograph will jog a memory or two of certain readers.

Holidaymakers shiver on the Whitley Bay rocks. The 1930s swimwear came in handy! These people also appear later on in the book.

This page of recommended hotels and boarding houses available in the early 1930s shows just how low normal wages were at the time.

Recommended Hotels and Boarding Houses

	Bed and Breakfast each person	Full Board each person
Waverley Hotel (Headquarters), Promenade	9s. 6d.	15s.
Avenue Hotel, Promenade	10s.	15s.
Hotel Esplanade, Promenade	8s. 6d.	12s. 6d.
The Royal Hotel, Promenade	7s. 6d.	11s. 6d.
St. Abbs, Promenade	5s. 6d.	8s. 6d.
Haven Hotel, Promenade	7s. 6d.	9s.
Parkhurst, Marine Drive	—	7s. 6d.
Kensington Hotel, Promenade	6s. 6d.	9s.
Y.W.C.A., Promenade	4s., 5s.	—
Esplanade Boarding House, Promenade	5s., 6s.	7s., 8s.
Mrs. Thornton, 50 Ventnor Gardens, Monkseaton	5s.	9s.
Mrs. Banks, 32 Percy Road, W. Bay	5s.	—
Mrs. Haswell, 3 Styan Av., W. Bay	7s. 6d.	12s. 6d.
Bay Hotel, Cullercoats	7s. 6d.	10s. 6d.

On the Sands, Whitley Bay

Children play on Whitley Sands *c.*1897. Note the beach huts behind. This postcard is perfect for picture framing as it says all there is to say about a peaceful, bygone time.

Splashing about in the sea, with a couple of boats in the background. Some of the people here are featured in the earlier photograph in this chapter.

A popular seafront shop selling tobacco and cigars. Above is the Manor House Café, *c.*1927.

A lonely but tranquil stroll along Whitley Bay Northern Promenade. Whitley Bay appears out of season here, but there are a few visitors. It may have been a normal working weekday.

Droves of holidaymakers on a sunny day outside The Empire. The ladies must have been boiling hot in their tight, thick fabric dresses, blouses and skirts. It was not quite the time to 'strip off' to their shirts and T-shirts to let the air circulate!

The construction of the Spanish City by contractors S.F. Davidson and Miller of Newcastle upon Tyne. This rare photograph demonstrates the simplicity of the dome's design.

A wet day on the Whitley Bay Promenade in the 1930s. Probably more people were present before the sudden downpour.

Before St Mary's Lighthouse was built, *c*.1890. Tracks in the sand have been made by a recently-departed boat. There are many stories surrounding what is essentially a small innocuous island. Most of the tales involve tragedy, smugglers and even murder. St Mary's Island was once a smugglers' paradise. So the story goes, contraband goods were transferred into small boats from a lugger and run into a deep winding gully called Smuggler's Creek on the north side of the island. They were quietly landed.

St Mary's Lighthouse and Island in all its glory, *c.*1910. Probably the worst sea tragedy ever to take place on here occurred on 7 April 1810. Several cobles of fishermen from Cullercoats were hit by a storm off Hartley. Blyth lifeboat put out to sea with a crew of 18, rowed its way through the storm and rescued 11 men. Returning home near the island's rocks, a huge wave engulfed the lifeboat, throwing all aboard into the sea. Out of 28 men only two survived, while the remainder perished in the freezing waters.

The South Promenade end of Whitley Bay, with its massive paddling pool. There were two camps of people, those who loved their outdoor swimming and those who found it unhygienic, especially as the years passed and the pool became rusty and dirty.

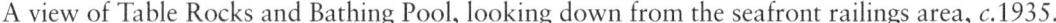

You will not find as many people as this on the North Promenade, even in the summer months. Groups do gather down here on Bonfire Night, to witness the fireworks display put on by the local council. It's a brief visit and there is not much change out of a few thousand pounds!

A view of Table Rocks and Bathing Pool, looking down from the seafront railings area, *c.*1935.

A stroll along the Whitley Bay Promenade provides this old gentleman with a breath of fresh air in the early 1930s. Over the years various rest homes have sprung up in the seaside town. And note the absence of Grant's Clock – it had yet to be erected!

An aerial view possibly taken from a window of the Waverley Hotel, now the Rex Hotel. Probably taken in the late 1920s to early 1930s.

The Express Gardens and Cenotaph, late 1940s. Taken from the height of Spanish City Dome allows the viewer to get an advantage sight of the effective dartboard design made from the flowers.

This hand-painted photograph of Whitley Bay sands is commonly used in framed pictures. When it's blown up in full colour it is really quite effective and could be mistaken for an oil painting.

Whitley Gala, 1913, attracts officials, scouts, children, adults and a policeman seen on the far left. The upturned box underneath the cart belonged to Bassett and Co. Confectionery. Within 12 months many of the men pictured here would have received their call-up papers from the draft board. World War One drew close.

A mother and her child sit on a bench in 1900, when The Avenue Hotel was still at its height of popularity and splendour.

A snow storm hits tea and food restaurant Panama House, belonging to Stephen Fry. And, not surprisingly, there's not a customer in sight.

A cycle trip to the Links, around 1920. This area became renowned for fish wives selling crabs and later on, fishcakes.

THE LINKS, WHITLEY BAY.

A picnic on the grass of the Links in about 1895. Once again, this is another type of 'people photograph' which makes for an effective framed picture.

The renamed Rex Hotel in 1938. Advertisements described the Rex as being the ideal place for a grand summer holiday with its 150 bedrooms – accommodation fit for 200 guests. And it is still going strong today, over 70 years on. The outbreak of World War Two was to disrupt business for many years until the late 1940s.

Whitley Bay Sunken Gardens *c.*1947. Hoping to attract the attention of smokers, a huge advertisement for Puck Matches is inescapable and would be very politically incorrect in 2007.

How the Spanish City looked in the 1950s in this postcard retrieved from a bring and buy sale in 1999.

A delightful postcard such as this would have been sent out during the 1930s. It is unusual in the sense that it does not show a typical coastal scene. Instead, the postcard maker has chosen a picture of the Briar Dene and surrounded it with flowers. The amorous sentiment signifies it was designed especially to send from one loved one to another.

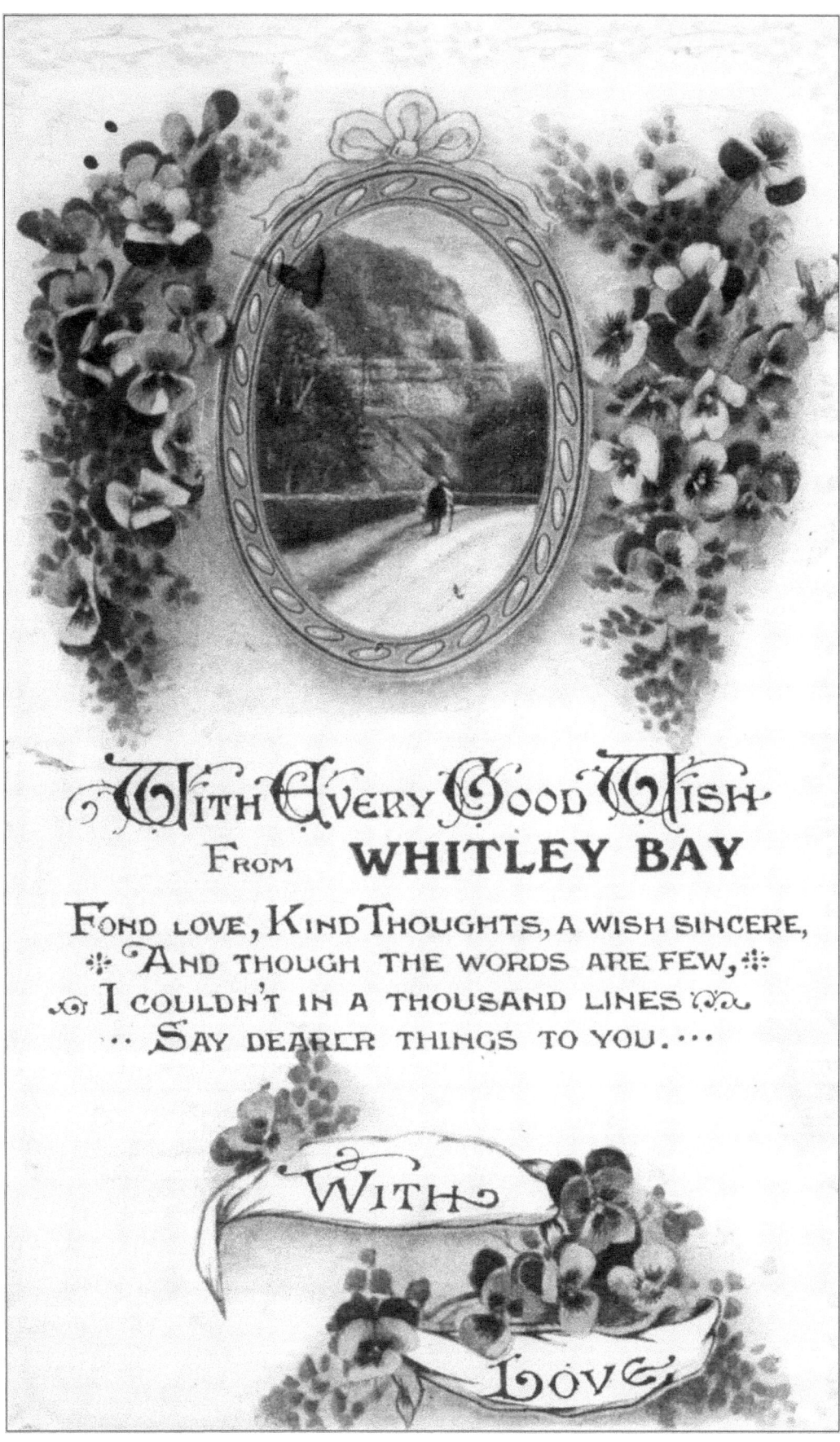

With Every Good Wish From **WHITLEY BAY**

Fond love, Kind Thoughts, a wish sincere,
And though the words are few,
I couldn't in a thousand lines
Say dearer things to you.

With Love

Whitley Bay was once described by a gentleman called William Rowling as being 'a historic Northumberland Town, easily accessible from all parts of the United Kingdom. From London to Edinburgh.' He mentions this part of the coast as being 'practically flat, no fatiguing climbs in any direction are necessary, an advantage to many including the elderly mobility affected'.

Children enjoy the company of the donkeys on the sands a century ago. William Rowling was also impressed by such sights. He continues, 'First impressions of Whitley count for much, and the visitor walking down to the golden flash of sands is greeted by charming children on donkeys, and dogs mildly barking; with families galore, enjoying the charm of the sea and the salty fresh air.'

THE SANDS, WHITLEY BAY.

This excellent postcard is a favourite among enthusiasts. Writer Mary Reed was also keen to express her thoughts about such a vision. 'It is a pure joy to get away from the stress of daily life, to stroll down to Whitley beach. The very name conjures up a summer vacation, blue skies and mild fresh air. The joy of witnessing others bathing and in small boats. And indeed, every breeze bears health upon its wings.' Very poetic!

A calm postcard from the 1920s showing the Spanish City 'out of season', but still the occasional visitor arrived.

The early 1980s saw the very expensive Cork Screw ride being constructed in the grounds of the Spanish City. It was meant to bring in the crowds, but despite the initial excitement people soon lost interest. It was then removed at a financial loss.

The construction of the Spanish City funfair in 1909 made it one of the most well-known landmarks in the north east. However, neglect and lack of use for its original purpose, i.e. as an entertainment centre, made it ugly and unpopular.

PADDLING AT WHITLEY BAY.

Paddling on the Whitley Bay shore 100 years ago. You will find marine life and vegetation among the small rocks at low tide, including long, fantastic fronds of emerald and olive-coloured seaweed. Hence, the location of the Dove Marine Laboratory in Cullercoats.

The Express Ballroom was a meeting place and a chance to have a dance. Like most seaside attractions it was of its time and as a result it became less popular with the young people who as the 1960s approached, favoured discos and nightclubs as entertainment.

The south end Promenade of Whitley Bay *c*.1904. From his 1936 diary, F.R. Carroll wrote, 'Looking seawards, an ever-changing picture presents itself, for there is an unending procession of merchant liners, coasting vessels, yachts, and fishing cobles passing to and fro. Shorewards the Promenade is fronted by fine hotels, cafés, and places of entertainment.'

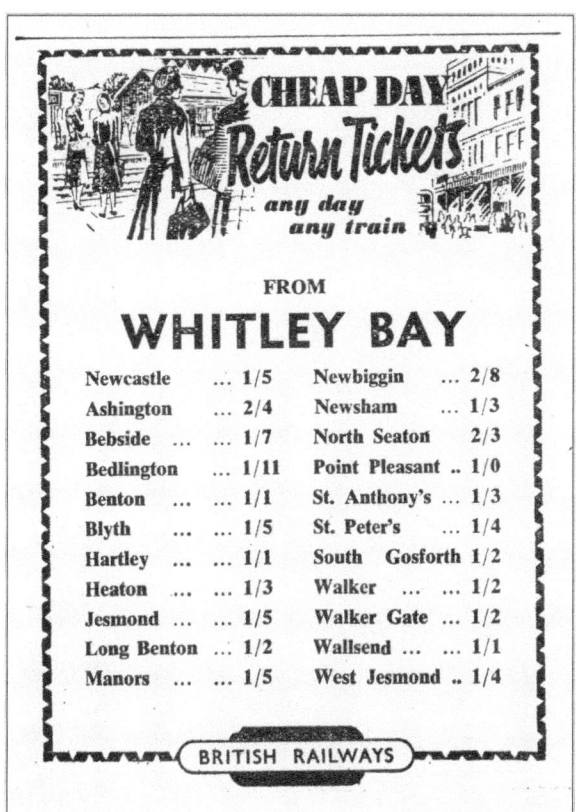

CHEAP DAY
Return Tickets
any day
any train

FROM

WHITLEY BAY

Newcastle	... 1/5	Newbiggin	... 2/8
Ashington	... 2/4	Newsham	... 1/3
Bebside ...	... 1/7	North Seaton	2/3
Bedlington	... 1/11	Point Pleasant	.. 1/0
Benton ...	... 1/1	St. Anthony's	... 1/3
Blyth ...	... 1/5	St. Peter's	... 1/4
Hartley ...	... 1/1	South Gosforth	1/2
Heaton ...	... 1/3	Walker ...	... 1/2
Jesmond ...	... 1/5	Walker Gate	... 1/2
Long Benton ...	1/2	Wallsend ...	... 1/1
Manors ...	... 1/5	West Jesmond	.. 1/4

BRITISH RAILWAYS

A British Railway poster for cheap-day returns from Whitley Bay, dated June 1954.

A moment of deep thought. Two ladies pay their respects to dead soldiers at the Whitley Bay Cenotaph.

The Hotel Esplanade was originally built in Edwardian splendour in 1908. It ran well for 90 years but was refurbished and reopened in 1998 – to a modern, high-quality standard. Magnificent sea views are available from many rooms as well as a first floor restaurant. Today, it resembles one of the more moderate buildings found in southern seaside resorts such as Eastbourne and Brighton.

ROCKS.
WHITLEY·BAY

A watercolour painting of the rocks at Whitley Bay found its way on to a postcard. The artist, however, is unknown.

Tucking into a nice picnic. A group of ladies from the 'typing pool' enjoy a day out at Whitley Bay, *c*.1932. The photograph was taken adjacent to the area known as the Feathers' Caravan Site, not far from St Mary's Island.

The Waverley Hotel in all its glory facing the sea elements in this old postcard.

The Monkseaton Bowling Green, also known as Souter Park, *c*.1955. And it's still there in 2007. What an achievement!

Percy Road in 1986. Originally built in 1873 for the middle classes, the properties were later owned by landlords and landladies and rented out as bed and breakfasts. One became a rest home.

This is one of Whitley Bay's first public sale rooms. Built entirely from wood, with a felt roof, it was situated on Whitley Road, with the proprietor during 1900 being a Mr George Bennison. Mr Bennison prided himself on his own adage that his place could provide the buyer with every household item imaginable, all at reasonable prices.

REX

(Formerly WAVERLEY)

HOTEL

WHITLEY BAY

The REX HOTEL, Whitley Bay, is the ideal place for a grand Summer Holiday. Situated on the Promenade facing the sea, it has 150 bedrooms (accommodation for 200 guests), private suites with complete toilet, and H. & C. in all New Wing bedrooms.

The Dining Room, Lounges and Buffet are roomy and comfortable: the excellent cuisine leaves nothing to be desired. For your amusement indoors there are two billiard rooms and a full-size table for table tennis, while in the evening, guests flock to the ballroom (with its new floor), where a first-class orchestra makes dancing delightful. Central Heating is installed throughout the Hotel. Two Tennis Courts. Garage for 50 cars. Car Park for 100 cars.

The Hotel is Fully LICENSED.

A.A.   ***   R.A.C.

N.B.—The change of name has not involved any change of ownership or management.

Resident Manager : KENNETH C. CRAIG.

Telephone: Whitley Bay 326-7.   Telegrams: 326 Whitley Bay.

An advertisement for the Rex Hotel. The manager, Mr Kenneth C. Craig, made it plain that the change of name did not involve a change of ownership.

Crofton's Café was situated on Whitley Road and is seen here in about 1900. As well as selling tea, coffee, breakfast and dinner, Crofton's also sold a variety of confectionery, especially Cadbury's and Fry's chocolate and drinks. Cyclists were allocated space at the back of the café where they could park their bicycles. Crofton's also had premises in Blackett Street, Newcastle upon Tyne.

Here we see the Carlton Café in all its magnificence. Situated on the promenade, it was in a prime location to attract holidaymakers. Overlooking the sea, it was said its teas and level of service were unsurpassed. All that remained of the Carlton building at the compilation of this book was barren land.

Gowanbrae, at 30 Windsor Crescent, was the guest house of Mrs Emma Coulson. In the 1936 *Whitley Bay Guide* the establishment was described as a dwelling with good homely apartments and excellent combined rooms. It sought to provide every home comfort away from home. With hot water, a wireless (radio) tuned to the BBC programme, a proper bath, piano and a lovely sea view, Gowanbrae was the perfect choice among holidaymakers. Board and residence cost two guineas per week.

Mrs Wylie's Guest House on 43 South Parade advertised a 'good home with well-earned reputation for comfort and service'.

Whitley Sands, 1953. Before the downward slide, people came to Whitley Bay in their droves. The sands would often be packed with families, all vying for a treasured part of the beach on which to lay their towels and get down to some serious sunbathing. You could not move for folk. But everyone loved it. With cheap foreign package holidays on offer today, scenes such as this one are hardly likely to be repeated. A sign of the times.

The Promenade Gardens, Whitley Bay, c.1930. Local resident James Garland recalls riding his cycle round here when he was growing up in the 1930s. The authorities were very strict about riding on the grass, so much so he had his ear clipped a few times by passing policemen! James said 'They couldn't do that now, but it kept us in line in those days!'

PROMENADE GARDENS, WHITLEY BAY.

June Hutton recalls New Year's Day down on the seafront of Whitley Bay in 1933. 'Just like this picture, we'd all get dressed up in the early morning in our best clothes and go down to the beach, or watch from the promenade those brave souls taking a dip in the "new year water". I don't know why they did it, or why they continue to do it. But it's good fun nevertheless!'

The scorching hot summer of 1976 sent temperatures soaring. The tale goes that 'you could cook an egg on the pavement'. The author's father, also called John Alexander (or 'Jack' to his friends), is seen here on Whitley Bay beach, slapping on the tanning oil.

Apparently the boy in this picture is still alive and living in Whitley Bay. He allowed the use of his photograph of him as a child playing in the sand with his toy vehicle. However, he wished not to be named. A box of a few of these old toys recently sold at a local auction sale for £300.

Dogs really suffered in the extreme heat of 1976. The family pet, Hector, was eager to do some paddling in the sea to keep cool.

Ship ashore! Well not exactly, but you can't fail to notice a ship or boat on the horizon from the promenade, as no doubt this lady and gentleman are doing in this picture from the early 1930s.

Whitley Bay seafront long ago. A mass of people enjoying themselves on a bank holiday.

Watt's Café during the mid-1970s. Families and children at play on the beach. The writing on the wall, however, looks terrible!

All children like the donkey rides, although this boy does not look too pleased. Maybe he's worried the donkey might bolt and he will fall off!

This is a familiar sight. As the tide came in, families would move further up the beach. This close up of the beach in 1930 shows these people are not far from the wall!

A grainy holiday snap inside the grounds of the Spanish City. The background is a painting and the donkey is not real.

Boys in 1905 on Whitley Rocks, with one looking upward to St Mary's Lighthouse. What a grim-faced bunch.

A holiday snap of the lighthouse from 1962. The picture was taken by Ted Grundy, who, as a keen artist, painted the scene, framed it and mounted it on the wall.

Station Road long ago, and not as busy as it usually was. It's remarkable how unchanged this vision is 100 years on.

Whitley Bay Sand Castle Competitions were commonplace for the first half of the 20th century.

Local resident Tom Miller has an old letter from his grandfather sent in 20 March 1919, which reads 'Visited Whitley today. The fresh sea air should do well to cure my chesty cough, for I am made joyful I will now see out the year.' And Mr Miller's grandfather did last out the year. He died in 1958 aged 87! Lots of people during this period put a lot of faith in natural methods to regain their health. Fresh air, hot steamy, salty baths etc, were all seen to rejuvenate the body.

A local resident recalls all her family going to the Spanish City funfare. Joan Roberts said 'The best thing was the ghost train. It was not really all that scary but it was very atmospheric. I loved the seaside candy rock too. Whitley Bay was a great place to grow up in and the Spanish City was this magical world we poor children could escape to.'

The old railings on the Whitley Bay Promenade, with the ever-present Waverely Hotel to the left.

Another hand-painted postcard of The Sands. Unlike with computers today where most things can be done with the press of a key, such work was for the experienced and steady-handed artists only.

Out for a stroll, or pushing a pram, or a car drive in the late 1920s or early 1930s.

This man has obviously caught sight of a postcard photographer and decided to straighten his tie and say 'cheese'. These sun and rain shelters were beautifully designed and were situated in various locations around the town. This one was on the promenade, in front of The Avenue Hotel.

The grounds of the Spanish City look like they are holding some sort of festival, as an area of ground appears to have been cleared for some reason.

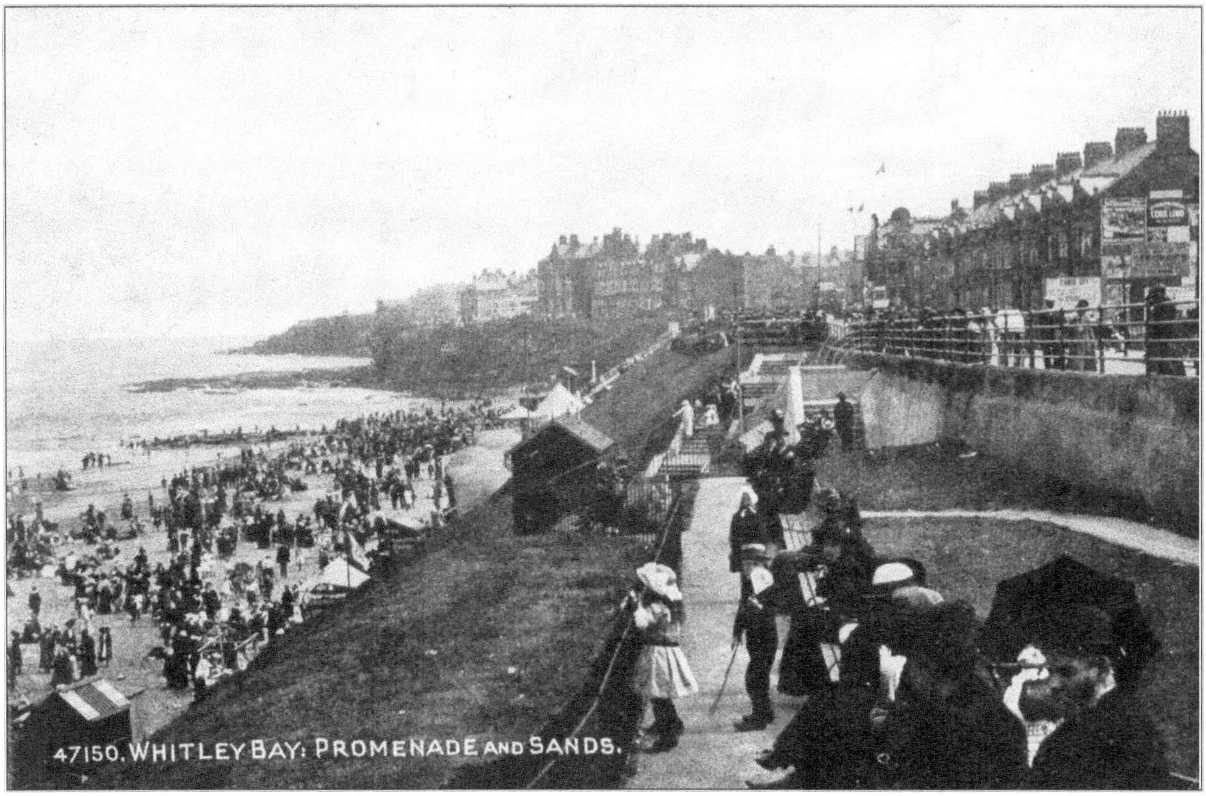
47150. WHITLEY BAY: PROMENADE AND SANDS.

This is one of the most commonly-viewed postcards of old Whitley Bay. It actually looks much better blown up into a framed picture than it does as a small photograph.

The Links in Whitley Bay. The road signs may be hard to read but they are directing traffic to the A192 and A193.

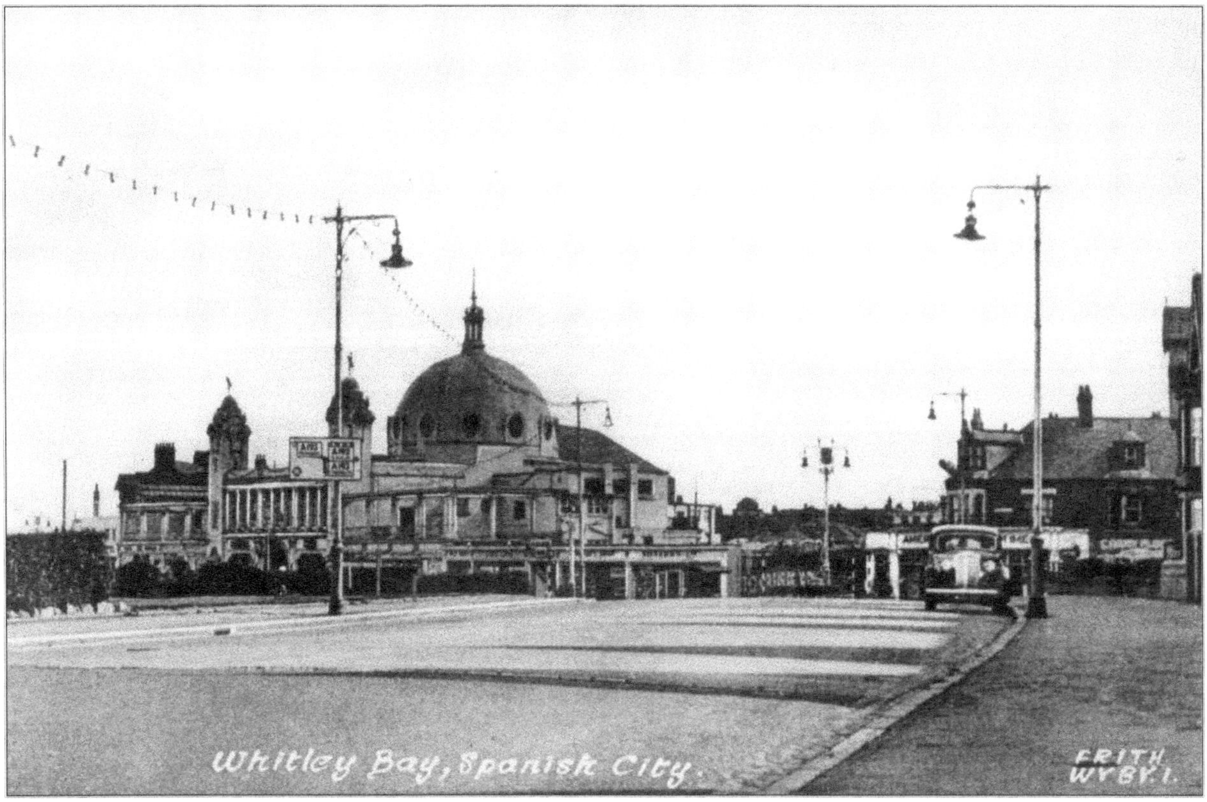
Whitley Bay, Spanish City.
FRITH WYBY.1.

This is another old, familiar postcard from over a century ago. The mass of people on the sands, the beach huts, all the activity taking place really does not do the picture justice in a small photograph such as a postcard. Like the one before, it has to be blown up quite large to be able to fully appreciate what's in the picture.

Although Whitley Bay has been through some rough times, with horrible boarded up and bricked up derelict buildings spoiling the landscape, this area has always been kept tidy and the grass kept neatly cut.

Swimming baths at Table Rock. There is one version of this postcard which was coloured in, but it's rare. This is the original black and white version. But the gentleman or lady who did the coloured version carried out this work well, the water tones in particular being the hardest to paint.

Children at play at the Panama Dip during the early 1950s. Note the deck chairs, which were also available to be hired for a few pennies.

CHAPTER THREE

Shows, People and Adverts

This publicity picture was taken in 1938. The Lyric Juveniles were a Whitley Bay group who treaded the boards at local shows and events. Because funds were low, friends and family made the costumes and they had some help financially from sponsors.

Another picture from 1938. This time the ladies are older and their costumes more daring. These 10 beauties made up The Lyric Girls and made regular appearances at The Priory Theatre. They were also asked to perform in South Shields, where they were equally popular both as a group and individually.

The under 10 to 12-year-olds were The Lyric Tots. Some may be alive today, in which case they would be nearing 80 years old.

A play of some sort and the costumes could not be more diverse. From left to right, Philip T. Cable, Ronnie Symington and Yvonne Bertham.

Empress Ballroom

***

DANCING & WHIST DRIVES
MONDAY, WEDNESDAY, SATURDAY
8 to 12 p.m. - - Admission 1/-
GEORGE CLIFFORD AND HIS BAND

***

SUNDAY EVENINGS at 8-0
Admission 6d.

CAFE CONCERTS with STAR ARTISTS
AND REG. FISHER AND HIS BAND

***

For Your Party or Dance — The Rotunda Suite. Comfort and Beauty Combined

An advertisement for the Express Ballroom, still providing entertainment in 1939 despite the war mongering of German Chancellor Adolf Hitler.

Harold L. Clunie plays Sergeant Malone in a comedy play entitled *Rounding Up*, written by Alan Hunt and staged in 1933. It was probably never performed again.

It's an odd tradition in British pantomime that the leading men are played by ladies! And this is no exception. From left to right, Margery Warren as Cinderella and Maureen Lorrimer as the Prince, *c.*1935.

Hand in hand and like two peas in a pod, Tweedle Dum and Tweedle Dee played by Derek Reed and Peter Bond.

TED BATEY as "DAME TROT"

Teddy Batey carved a niche playing pantomime dames – here he is in 1937 as Dame Trot. He was said to have been influenced by the comic act at the time, Old Mother Riley.

The attractive beaming face of Mona Ragg in the role of Jack (Jack and the Beanstalk). Mona was an amateur actress in Whitley Bay, but what was her day job? If you are a relative of Mona the author would like to hear from you.

The Money Lender played by Harold Field looks like he has got some inspiration from Hollywood actor James Finlayson, who starred at the time in many Laurel and Hardy shorts.

An autographed
pictured of acclaimed
boxer Teddy Rollins
was sent to a fan in
Whitley Bay.

Here's another local
actress. Ethel Brander
played Amy Jewitt in
a local stage
production in 1933.

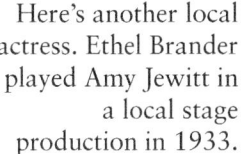

Leon Dodd's Super Entertainers regularly performed on the Links Bandstand Pavilion. They are pictured here in 1938, trumpets, saxophone and drum at the ready.

Whitley Bay amateur actors gather in full costume in 1907 for a show involving Scots, maids, a dandy, fishwives, the British Army and a sheikh!

Simply known as 'The Manager', this fellow's real name is unknown but his picture is credited to a production of a play called *The Willow's Nest*, staged in Whitley Bay on 14 June 1929.

Leon Dodd's Super Entertainers in 1936. Different musicians were added from time to time to add spice and variety to the performances – not that this was necessary, as they were said to bring the house down.

Little Miss Tweedy, a pantomime 'dolly', frequently performed by local thespian Jane Blackburn.

The Whitley Bay Playhouse, pictured here in here in the early 1990s. As well as showing movies, guest stars, including comedian Ken Dodd, have performed here for many years.

Celebrated
television, radio
and stage star
Hannah Gordon
appeared at the
Whitley Bay
Playhouse in the
late 1990s.

Drag queen comedy double act
Hinge (George Logan) and Bracket
(Patrick Fyffe) made frequent visits
to the Whitley Bay Playhouse.
Accompanied on the piano by Dr
Evadne Hinge, the elderly duo
treated audiences to old-fashioned
musical evenings from their home
in Stackton Tressell where both
sang selections from light operetta,
musical comedies and the works of
Noel Coward and Ivor Novello.
Sadly, Patrick died in 2002.

The late, respected, all-round actor Peter Barkworth performed at the Playhouse too, in the late 1990s.

Thirteen-year-old boys from Whitley Bay Grammar School in Hollywell Avenue, in full costume for their 1956 stage production of a play called *The Stolen Prince*.

Children enjoy a mock wedding for their school play at Park School (or Coquet School) in 1955.

'The audience is the other way!' should have been the cry when this picture was snapped at an operatic show in Whitley Bay in 1963.

Rockcliffe School hosted this musical called *The Japanese Bride* in October 1958. Either the school leaving age had radically gone up or the teaching staff and parents decided to put on a performance for the children.

The old people's home on the Links enjoy some kind of festive mirth at this Christmas party in 1953. This is one of few pictures known to be taken inside the home.

Four ladies sit on chairs, fundraisers at the same old people's home's Christmas party in 1953.

Whitley Bay is renowned for its eateries and apparently this was the place to enjoy a fine evening of food, Meluilles Bistro in North Parade. The advert is dated 1966.

A publicity still from an amateur production of a play called *Thinking Aloud*, written in 1948 by a Whitley Bay lady called Mary Watts.

PRIORY PAVILION, WHITLEY BAY
Telephone 319
The New Production by Mr. Eddie Morrell.

'Starlights of 1948'
AT 7-15 p.m. DAILY.
Matinees 2.30 p.m. Wednesdays (and in wet and inclement weather).

Special Sunday Performances at 8 p.m. (Matinees if wet or inclement at 3 p.m.).

PROGRAMME No. 2
"HAME TAE THE GLEN"
Showing Monday to Wednesday, July 12—14

PROGRAMME No. 4
"YE OLD MUSIC HALL"
Showing Thursday to Saturday, July 15—17

See announcements of future programmes in this paper.

Prices of admission:— Evenings: 3/-, 2/6 and 1/9
(Children under 14 if accompanied by an adult 1/6, 1/3 and 1/-.)
Matinees: 2/6, 2/- and 1/6
(Children under 14 accompanied by an adult 1/3 and 1/-.)

Booking Office open:—
Between 9.30 a.m.—12.30 p.m. and 2 p.m.—5.30 p.m.
Sundays, 2 p.m.—5.30 p.m.

Do Not Miss The Beautiful Fluorescent Scenes

The Priory Theatre presents *Starlights of 1948*, a new production at the time by a gentleman called Eddie Morrell.

Most people can get an acting role without even trying. This chap appeared as The Friendly Giant in a production called *On The Green Hill*. Apparently, reference is made to this chap being over 6ft 5in tall.

An apparently little known event called Whitley Bay's Beautiful Tot Contest 1935, with contestant Michael Reed coming fourth!

A display of usual cars of their time on the Links saw this odd vehicle being parked up in an early forerunner to the Whitley Bay Motorshow, *c.*1950.

This picture has been chosen to go in the book for no other reason than these twins look happy in their oversized pram. The picture was discovered at a house clearance in Whitley Bay in 1989.

Playing the slot machine bandits inside the Spanish City in 1952. Nothing complicated, just pull the handle and see if you win.

This old man from Whitley Bay has been featured in a book once before. To our knowledge no person came forth to identify him. He is certainly a curious-looking fellow who is tall enough to be nearly the same height as the others while sitting down.

Local actress Nancy
Page in full costume for
her role as Wanda in
The Princess Slept,
1932.

A council pageant along the Whitley Bay seafront in late
1977 brought the crowds out.

A scene being filmed behind camera of the 1978 Thames ITV serial *Funny Man*, starring Jimmy Jewel and Lynda Bellingham.

You are probably too young to have ever ridden on the Joy Wheel, but it's reported that it was like a giant 78 record spinning at speed.

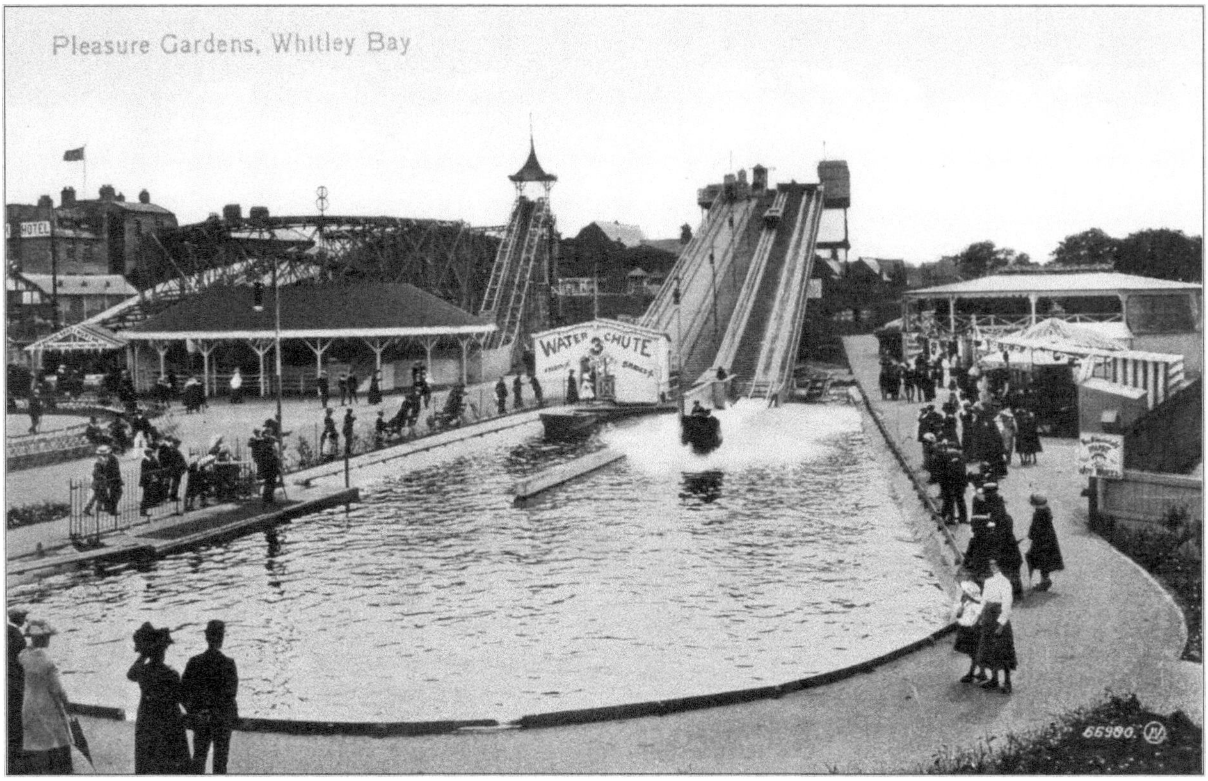
Pleasure Gardens, Whitley Bay
WATER CHUTE
66980.

Like the Joy Wheel, the Water Chute was another popular funfare attraction. It looks a thrill of a ride.

Bradley Marsh is seen here building a snow man in the back of Hollywell Avenue in 1963. Shame it melted.

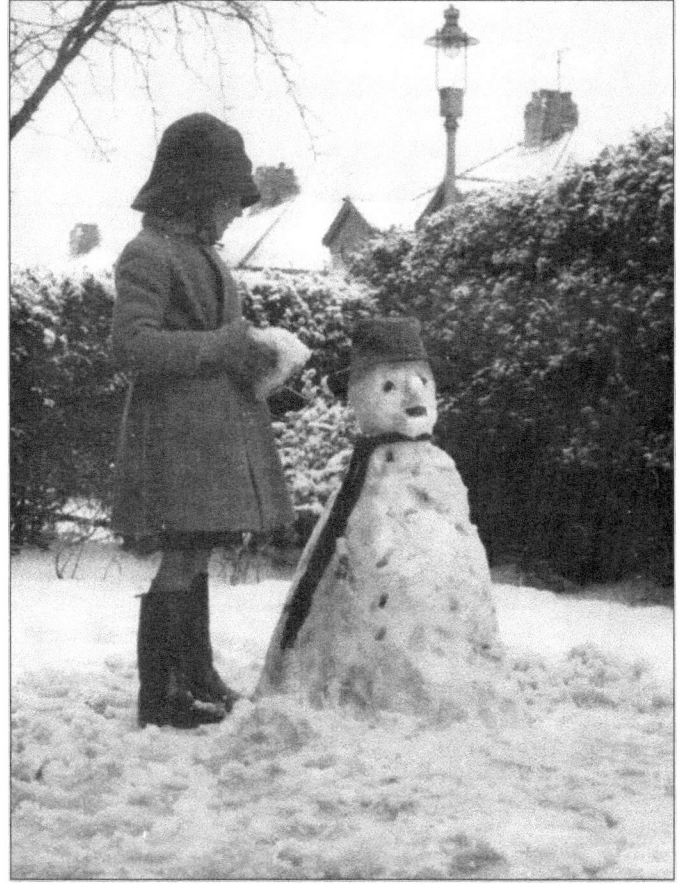

The Ship pub on Whitley Road in 1977. The gentleman with the glasses is Andy Moore and his daughter, Evelyn Moore, is on the far right. The rest are bar staff and caterers.

More bar staff at The Ship pub in 1977. Unfortunately, their names are unknown to us, but surely someone reading this will recognise them!

Bar staff and caterers in The Ship pub in Whitley Bay in 1977. Second from right is the author's mother, Eva Alexander, and standing next to her is her friend Vareena.

This is no digital photography. It's James Dean actually standing next to the author's mother, Eva Alexander. Well, really it's a classic cardboard cut-out from the 1950s, bought at J.C. Featonby Auctioneers on Park View.

The Whitley Bay Operatic Society

Formerly

WHITLEY, MONKSEATON AND DISTRICT
AMATEUR OPERATIC SOCIETY
(FOUNDED 1911)

Affiliated   *Operatic and*

to the National   *Dramatic Association*

WILL PRESENT

"GLAMOROUS NIGHT"

A ROMANTIC PLAY WITH MUSIC BY IVOR NOVELLO
(By arrangement with Messrs. Samuel French Ltd.)

IN THIS THEATRE

DURING THE WEEK Commencing 27th March

For particulars of Advance Booking Scheme
apply to the

Hon. Sec., H. A. HAWKINS,
53 Hartley Avenue,
Monkseaton;
Telephone: Whitley Bay 1327.

or

Hon. Treas., DAVID A. HARRIS,
23 Brier Dene Crescent,
Whitley Bay.
Telephone: Whitley Bay 850.

A poster advertising Whitley Bay Operatic Society's production of *Glamourous Night*, commencing on Monday 17 March 1939.

A theatrical publicity picture for a 1947 play called *Look into the Fire*, a curious play in which the photograph lives up to its title!

A small ceremony for a Drama and Music Teaching Award at Marden Bridge Middle School in the early 1950s, when it was a grammar school.

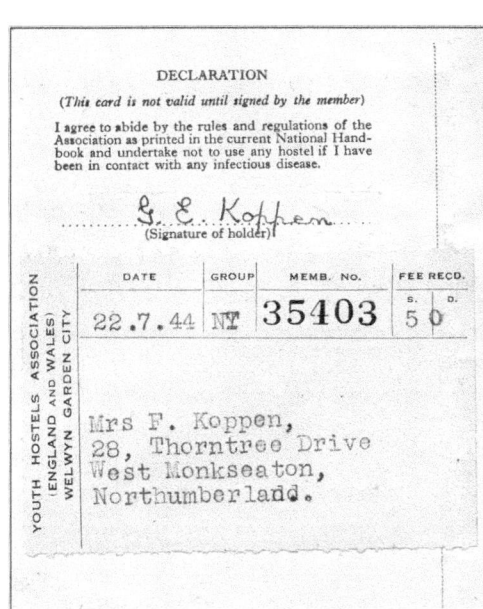

A 'Roving Hostels' card belonging to a Mrs F. Koppen of Thorntree Gardens, July 1944. It is unusual in that when War World Two was raging at its worst and coming to a climax, this Mrs Koppen was visiting hostels. Perhaps she was involved in the war effort.

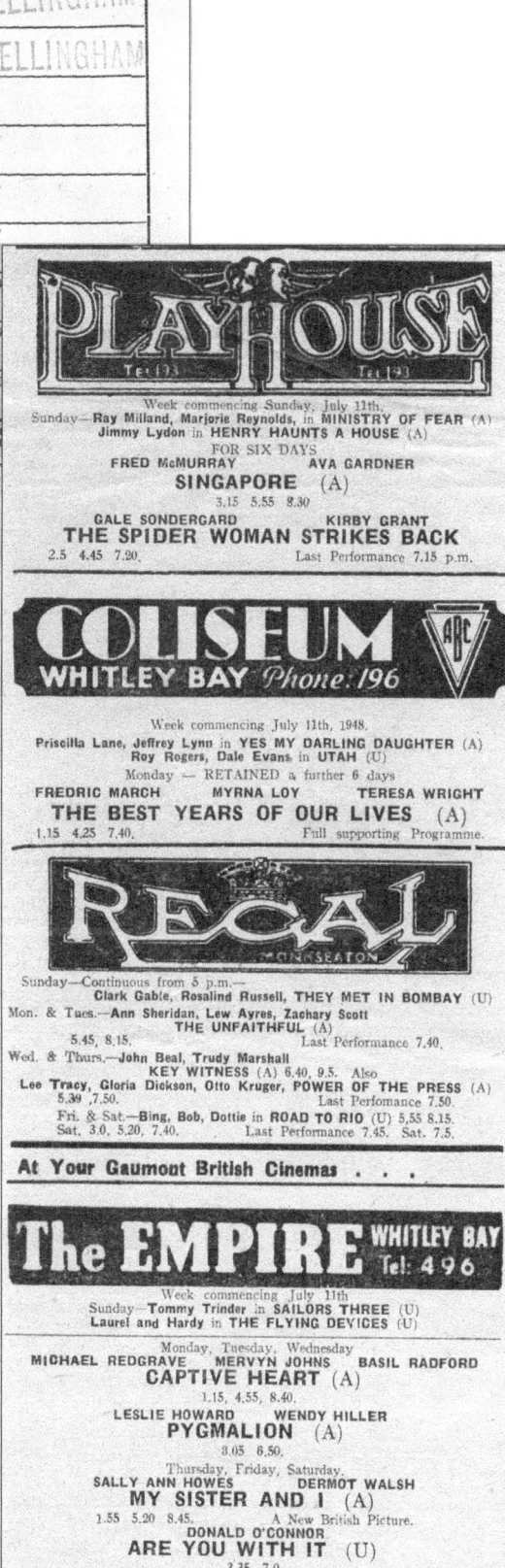

What the four leading cinemas where showing in July 1948. Among others, Fred McMurray and Ava Gardner in *Singapore*, and Michael Redgrave and Mervyn Johns in *The Captive Heart*.

This is the official Whitley Bay Coat of Arms, which was granted letters on 23 April 1954. Translation of the motto *Non sibi sed omnibus* means 'not for oneself but for all'.

In the vicinity of Tynedale Avenue, Whitley Bay, the picture is dated 19 July 1951. It's an interesting image of a Whitley Bay long gone.

Diddyman comedian Ken Dodd never short-changes the audience whenever he comes to Whitley Bay. Usually, doors are locked at 10pm – while you are still in the theatre! It's a joke his fans will understand, for his performances can go on until 1am!

June Page dancing merrily in a musical called *By the Light of the Moon*, staged in 1931.

HEALTHY COOKING
means HEALTHY COOKS

Switch to
ELECTRICITY

FOR DOMESTIC POWER HEATING AND COOKING

NOW ONLY $\frac{3^D}{4}$ PER UNIT

Oh for the merits of electricity! After being used to gas for so long, suddenly home users were asked to switch to electric to cook. This advert is from the *Whitley Seaside Chronicle*.

Alan Cook, known to some in Whitley Bay as 'Cookie'. He was a fundraiser and helped get funds together to stage productions.

Stephen Jardine and Sara Preece in a production called *The Lovelorn Soldier*, c.1934.

Harold Clunie both acted and was a support manager in theatre, but he mainly worked in South Shields. Here he is in 1929.

Opposite: An eat more fish campaign was launched in the 1940s, and Mr Edward Jones placed this magazine advertisement in order to drum up trade.

John Brooks was a bank clerk, who acted mainly without speaking dialogue.

This pet cat was not a star of stage, but a mice catcher in a bakery no longer around. It was taken in 1960, and the cat's name was Peril! The devil!

CHAPTER FOUR

Memories of Whitley Bay

Whitley Bay has seen numerous shops come and go, and mostly go over the last 100 years. From auctioneers, electric and gas shops, to television, furniture shops and bakeries. Few that start complete a two-year run, never mind last more than a decade. Carters and Finlays are two such shops which are still at the top, and have even expanded in the last 70 years. The family business found the key to success and look destined to be around for a few more decades yet.

Because Carters and Finlays are steeped in history and are as much a part of Whitley Bay as the Lighthouse or Spanish City, the next 12 images are dedicated to the families and their customers, who brought quality baking and decorating into the homes of Whitley and far yonder.

It all began over 100 years ago when John Henderson Findlay opened a shop at 28 Market Place, Blyth, selling paint, hardware and glass. In 1931 he opened a branch in Whitley Bay, at the older north end of Park View at number 331/333 (although having been renumbered since). A diary entry during 1933 indicated the business was known as 'Finlay & Sons', with the 'd' in Findlay having been dropped. This branch was run by his son, John Henderson (or Jack as he was known) and was assisted by his married sisters Mabel Barlow and Ada Ferris.

On 1 March 1936, as 'J.H. Finlay', Jack set out on his own, taking over the Whitley Bay business. The development at the south end of Park View in the 1930s brought an impressive row of new shops to Whitley Bay.

And with the success of the Finlays' paint shop and decorating business, Carters – a local independent baker and confectioner – was taken on in around 1955. The range of bread and cakes produced by Carters proved very popular. And despite competition from supermarkets, the business still flourishes today. The following 12 photographs show both Finlays and Carters over the years.

The bread strike in 1974 meant queuing up at Carters in Park View. The unoccupied premises on the right, previously a Laws supermarket, became the Halifax Building Society.

Jack Finlay pictured *c*.1942 in his war uniform and looking remarkably fit and young for 38 years old. He died in 1985.

Irene, from Seaton Delaval, serving in Carters in the 1950s. The cake, pie and bread display fittings have hardly changed.

Jack Finlay goes through the mail, behind the counter at Carters, during the mid-1960s.

Peter Finlay is happy to try to keep up with the heavy demand at Carters during the infamous bread strike in 1974, when flour was like gold dust.

Finlay's first vehicle was used to transport men and equipment. This photograph was taken at the bottom of Duke Street, Whitley Bay, near the local shop. And although the exact date is unknown, the sign on the side, Finlay and Sons, puts it between 1933 and 1936.

Mr J. Finlay with his team of decorators in 1938. This picture by Gladstone Adams of Station Road, Whitley Bay, was taken behind Park View shops. The high wall separates the men from Steel's Nurseries on the other side. Pictured back row, left to right are: unknown, unknown, unknown, unknown, Johnstone, unknown, John Henderson Finlay, Lee, unknown, unknown, John Reay, Leslie Stafford, unknown, H. Wylie, Curtis. Middle row: L. Mackin, unknown, Bill Finlay, Lee, Billy Usher, Cowdon, George Howe, Lee. Front row: unknown, unknown, Burrows, Cecil Usher, Bill Patterson, Jimmy Lockie.

Finlays' simple but traditional shop front in Park View, Whitley Bay, in October 1979.

Michael Finlay paints the surface of St Paul's Church clock blue. This picture dates between 1968 and 1972.

BLOTTER

Dont put it off — put it on!

EVERY year property owners are faced with repair bills through neglecting to repaint in time.

Does your house, garage, gate, fence or greenhouse need attention? We undertake house decoration and repairs of every description. It will cost you nothing to consult us.

WHITE OR COLOURED
LEAD PAINT LASTS

J H. FINDLAY & SONS
333, Park View, WHITLEY BAY
Phone: Whitley Bay 1123

Lead Paints Protect

E.7

Advertising is what helps pull in the customers, and Finlays have always opted for the class effect. This advert dates from between 1931 and 1936.

After World War Two, success over Adolf Hitler and his allies gave rise to this comical advertisement, with Winston Churchill giving the orders, *c.*1945–46.

IMPROVING THE SHINING HOUR

WE do not claim that our staff employ their luncheon hour quite as strenuously as our artist has suggested, but we are confident that no time will be lost in carrying out any redecoration which you give us the opportunity to undertake. May we suggest that you give us the chance at all events of quoting?

N.B.—You can now have White Lead Base Paints with a Hard Gloss finish.

WHITE LEAD PAINT LASTS
IN WHITE OR COLOURS
J. H. FINLAY
DECORATOR
28 PARK VIEW, WHITLEY BAY
(opposite St. Paul's Church)
'Phone : 1123

This advert can be dated from August 1936 to July 1938. The short telephone number consists of just four digits.

John (or Jack) Taylor lived for many years in Cullercoats. He was very fond of Shakespeare, especially *Richard II*. He tried but failed to get his own interpretation of the play staged in Whitley Bay in 1923, but other committee members thought it too long-winded for audiences. Taylor had suggested the play be cut up into three pieces, each one staged seven days apart.

Actor Jack Hetherington said nerves always got the better of him while on stage so he turned his hand to directing. In later years Wallsend-born Jack was often mistaken for horror actor Peter Cushing.

This man's name is unknown but he appeared to have links with the occasional opera piece. The photograph is dated October 1930.

Harold S. Dodds came from a leading theatrical family and had a keen eye for a successful production. He often preferred to stage unknown plays as opposed to the classics, because that way they would be greeted without the audience first having an opinion about them.

Roland Ash looks a bit stern in his glasses but he was said to have a good sense of fun. He was art director and also stage manager for numerous pantomimes and opera productions in the 1920s and 1930s.

Fred C. Innes was a producer of many stage productions just before World War Two. He also acted as chairman if need be and was always seen at an opening night with his dickie bow tie on.

Doctor R.M.C. Harris pictured in 1926 is actually only 28 years old in this picture. The beard makes him look older!

Local theatre manager Harry Hunter was a joint treasurer for many acting groups in the area in the mid 1930s.

At first it was thought this was a picture of a member of the aristocracy. He definitely has that air of authority about him. But not according to the back, for it says 'Michael Gorman, Whitley medic.' Go on, tell us it's a member of the Russian Royal Family!

Old business people remembered! W.L. Dowling was a moneybags who was also chairman of the Pitman Shorthand Reception Committee. He is seated here at Gladstone Adams Photographers in 1936.

BBC Radio Newcastle DJ Paddy McDee was formerly a bank clerk but moved into radio in the early 1970s. He joined Metro and made an appearance at The Whitley Bay Motor Show in 1977 on the Links, signing autographs. At the time he was wearing flares, platform shoes, an open-neck cheesecloth shirt and a medallion. Attire and accessories he would like to forget!

Two adverts from a 1948 leaflet popped through the door explaining the merits of saving money on water. One for a men's tailors R. Bolton Ltd, another for Teasdale Dairy on Park View, Whitley Bay.

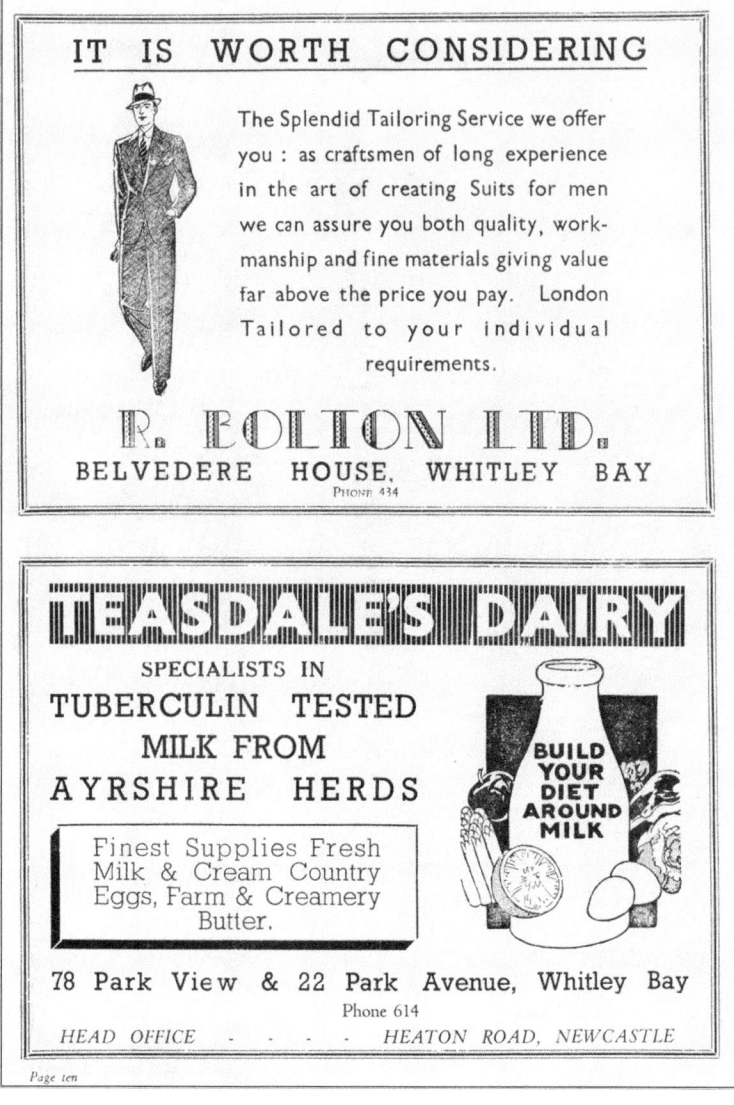

Local resident Paul Jenkins has memories of Whitley Bay and the BBC Radio One Roadshow. Paul said 'The Radio One Roadshow used to come every year to seaside places. I remember wanting to see a top star like Tony Blackburn or Noel Edmonds. It was sort of a pot luck who you got. They never seemed to come to Whitley Bay, until one year the Roadshow did, and they set up their turntables and speakers on the Links. I was elated but then disappointed. It was not my idea of a big star but a minor DJ who had a radio show at the weekend!'

Who remembers Michael Rodd from BBC television's *Tomorrow's World*? The star of 70s television also went to a Grammar School in Hollywell Avenue, Whitley Bay. Eva Alexander (the author's mother) worked there for a few years in the early 1970s. By then Michael had left school and was already famous. But Eva recalls the splendour of the building. 'It's a shame the school was knocked down.' The plot is now occupied by flats.

Nurses at a doctor's surgery in Whitley Bay. The exact location is unknown but on the back it says 'Whitley nurses'. Those overalls look more like they are made of tough material.

Likely Lads Rodney Bewes and James Bolam brought the screen version of their hit television sitcom to Whitley Bay in 1976. Here are the pair on set. Many scenes were filmed outdoors along the Links and near the Spanish City.

In 1988 Princess Diana was in Whitley Bay in July of that year and paid a visit to the Base Youth Centre in Esplanade, meeting the young and discussing their problems.

A fishwife at work selling crabs and fish at her stall in Whitley Bay.

Respected playwright Tom Hadaway lived a long time in Whitley Bay and loved his home in Marine Avenue.

Strictly on the Record !

We are happy to announce that we have now available a high Quality

PORTABLE RECORDING APPARATUS

Local Choirs, Orchestras, Singers, Children's Speech Training Classes, Public Speakers may now have High Fidelity Recordings made in their homes or studios at their own convenience.

A 5-inch record for messages for friends abroad to 13-inch record for orchestral items are available at moderate prices. Quotations given for any class of recording.

TOM S. FORD *Ltd*

Radio and Electrical Dealers,
184, PARK VIEW, WHITLEY BAY
Telephone 665

Our Associated Company, GEORGE SWAN (North Shields) LTD., recently recorded the combined Choirs at Festal Evensong at Christ Church, North Shields, great success.

For anything electrical, a visit to Tom S. Ford was a must. The shop in Park View was always where the latest technology was. From high-tech portable reel-to-reel tape recorders to the very latest 78 records! A large oversized radiogram was also a 'must have' in 1940.

Villa CARBONATED BEVERAGES

The family favourites:
VILLA LEMONADE 4½d
VILLA SARSAPARILLA 5d
3d Deposit on bottles

This delightful advert from the *Whitley Bay Guardian* in 1938 is just so cute. It's rare today for such advertising to be as innocent yet so ingeniously simple. A classic.

Before the 1970s brought heavy chipboard into our homes, shops like Bainbridge and Son in Park View sold real furniture made from real wood.

Artist Tony Hart (pictured) holds fond memories for Christine Davies, who, as a little girl, rang BBC television's *Swap Shop* in 1980 to ask the star to draw a horse for her. And he did, live on air. It was sent in a floppy 'do not bend' envelope which was duly creased in half when it was put through the letterbox. Eastbourne Gardens resident Christine treasured it. But, unfortunately, she lost it when she got married!

Auction Rooms have always turned unwanted goods into cash. Rawes at the top of Percy Road, on Whitley Road, was a hive of activity every Thursday for bidding. One regular remembers a funny line uttered by the auctioneer. When trying to flog a quality oak sideboard for 50p, the disgruntled man said 'Come on, the handles are worth more than that!'

During World War One, young men like this were drafted into the army with astonishing swiftness, classed as boys one day and men the next. Before they knew it they would be fighting for King and country. If they had sweethearts, a photograph would be kept close by. All the more poignant when news arrived home with the message 'lost in action'.

Soldiers and their mascots, a cat and dog, pose for a group photograph in 1917. Whitley Bay women bore their wartime experiences in both world wars with courage, while their husbands and sons (and daughters!) were engaged on the battle fronts. The measure of the town's military contribution, by those who paid the supreme sacrifice, is perpetuated by the inscriptions on the Link's Cenotaph.

During World War One there were shops from Beach Avenue to Holly Avenue, but from there to Marine Avenue was an open space where troops were drilled. On the opposite side of the street there were shops as far as Countess Avenue, and from that point to Marine Avenue was a field surrounded by a hedge. Makeshift hunts (one is pictured) were crudely erected using concrete and wood. They were pulled down shortly after Britain and her allies gained victory over the Germans in 1918.

This soldier was probably stationed at St Mary's Island in 1917, although during World War One the armed forces were everywhere. Unlike the previous picture of the hut, this one was taken by a professional photographer, possibly Gladstone Adams.

This picture simply says 'Marine Avenue, Whitley'. Are these soldiers standing in someone's back garden? The high wall and greenery would certainly suggest that. The board they are holding to the camera says 'St George for Merry England'.

In the region of what is now called 'Churchill Playing Fields', *c*.1916. It looks as if the soldiers are taking a relaxing break, but this is far from the truth. The army was constantly on alert. Even a seemingly peaceful situation could suddenly turn dangerously disruptive. On August Bank Holiday 1914, as a troop train was about to leave Whitley Bay Railway Station, a Zeppelin flew over in the darkness and dropped its bombs. The old gas company building in Whitley Road was destroyed and many houses in Albany Gardens were baldy damaged.

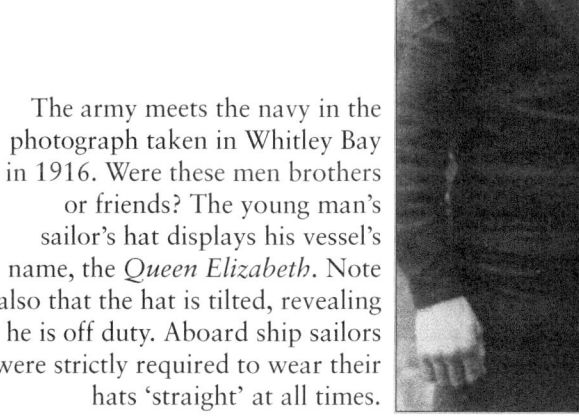

The army meets the navy in the photograph taken in Whitley Bay in 1916. Were these men brothers or friends? The young man's sailor's hat displays his vessel's name, the *Queen Elizabeth*. Note also that the hat is tilted, revealing he is off duty. Aboard ship sailors were strictly required to wear their hats 'straight' at all times.

Christmas, 1915.

While World War One raged on, some civilians sought solace in still being able to celebrate the festive season, but obviously without their menfolk by their sides. This is a typical Christmas card from 1915, which was probably purchased at one of the varied shops found on Whitley Road at the time.

Another classic advert from the pages of *The Whitley Bay Guardian*. This time from 1949 for Keiller's Little Chip marmalade.

INSIST ON Keiller's "Little Chip" Marmalade

– also KEILLER'S JAMS *they're delicious !*

Most areas are smokeless zones today, but back in 1948, as this advertisement from the *Whitley Seaside Chronicle* outlines, it did not matter how much smoke bellowed from the chimney. G.N. Straughton was a coal and coke merchant on Park View. They also sold fireplaces, grates and logs.

If this was 70 years ago, you could have got your dry cleaning done at Bradburn's in Station Road. Established in 1832, but no longer in business today.

Park School, May 1905. Younger primary school pupils mixed with older children.
On the opening day, 102 years ago, 686 boys and girls aged seven to 10 were present.

Rockcliffe School in 1927. Some of these were known to go off fighting in World War Two, but not to return. One who is still alive at the age of 90, when this book went to press, is Edmund Atkinson, pictured in the front row, third from left.

Rockcliffe School pictured here in 1982. Despite coming under the name Whitley Bay, it's slightly bordering on Cullercoats' territory.

Taken in 1894, this picture shows a class at St Paul's School, which used to stand at the foot of Norham Road. In the same building the first town meeting was held nearly 90 years ago. On the back of the photograph there is a recipe for a cold cure, which requires the poor patient to take one dessert spoon of sugar three times daily, washed down with quarter of a pint of hot water!

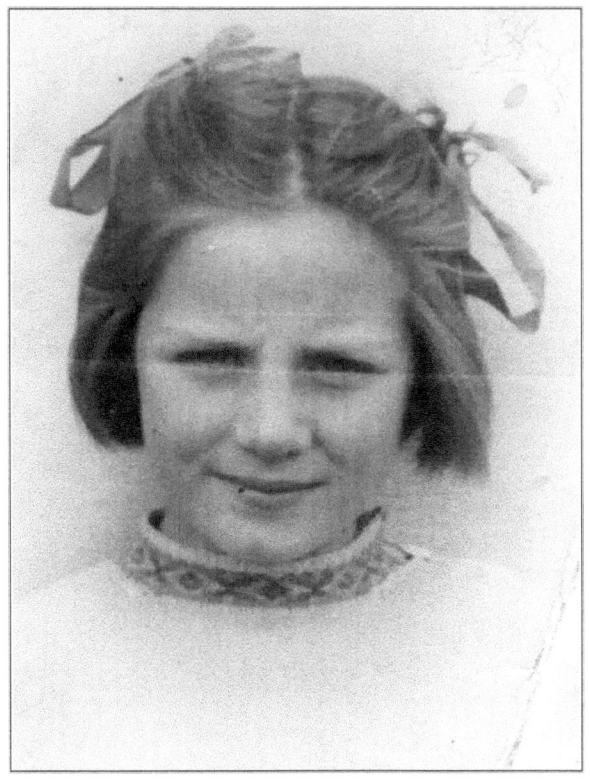

'Yes, can I help you, sir...madam?' That's how you would probably be greeted by these grim-faced shop assistants on Station Road.

Monkseaton resident Joan Utterson in 1946, aged eight. Joan has vivid memories of her life living by the coast. She got her first part-time job delivering newspapers. And she also remembers the worst snow fall ever, back in 1947. She was nine years old and attended Park School in Whitley Bay. She takes up the story. 'I can remember walking down to school and back every day for quite a time and the snow was up to my chest. I used to make pocket money by going around the neighbours, especially the elderly, every morning and shovelling the snow away with my homemade shovel-board my Dad made me. It was also the time that the Greek ship *Zephyros* went aground in between Whitley Bay and Cullercoats. It was quite an exciting time for everyone, crowds including myself would go and just stand and watch as it was firmly stuck on the rocks. My husband tells me he and friends, while ploughing their way through the deep snow to go and see the wreck, saw villagers standing around praying as the lifeboat prepared to launch in the stormy sea.'

Joan's father John William (or 'Billy') Potts was a stone mason. He laid the whole Promenade with flags in celebration of the 1951 Festival of Britain.

Three happy gentleman pose for their picture at 10 Promenade Studio, Whitley Bay.

'Photograph for Grandma' was on the back of this postcard. 'Dolly on her 16th birthday'. Just who was Dolly? And it begs the question, why is she not sitting in the chair?

No surname for this fashionable lady, all except 'All my love, from Norma.' Little did she know when this picture was taken some 100 years later it would be in a book.

Boys and girls from Bygate School, on Vernon Drive, Monkseaton, in a class first-year photograph.

This scene in reality was never to be. A Whitley Bay Pavilion to rival those found at such places as Eastbourne and Blackpool. It did not go ahead due to complications mainly involving cost.

This faded picture is of the Nettleton household (the author's relatives on his mother's side) in 1920. Pictured from left to right, Emily, Elizabeth, John, Jessie, Tommy and Esther Nettleton. Over the years the family lost trace of each other. John Nettleton (the author's grandfather) died aged 80 in 1977.

This is a receipt for Horseman's Garage which traded on Marine Gardens, Whitley Bay, for many years. The owner of the Ford car repaired lived at 28 Thorntree Drive. And the total cost of the bill was just £1.90!

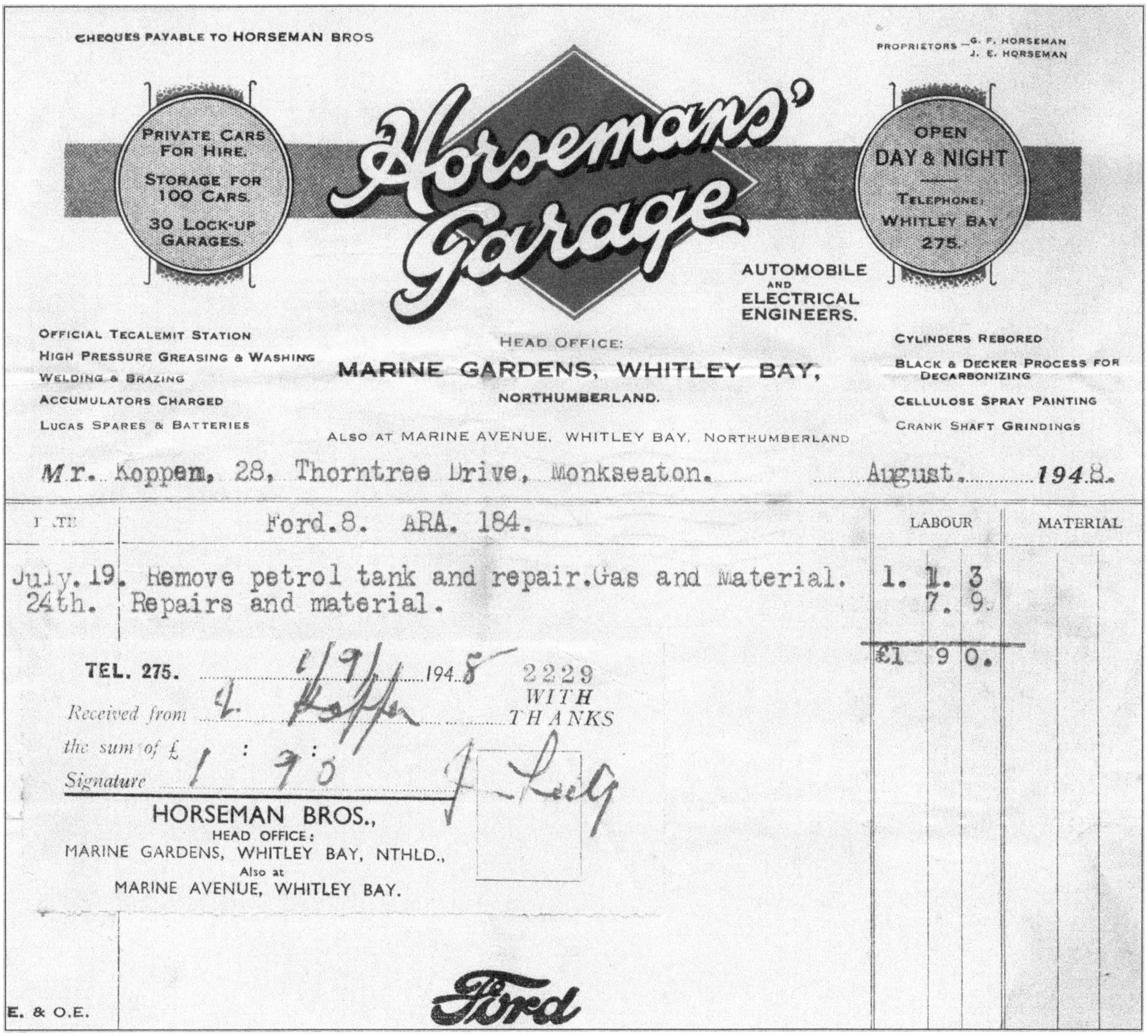

CHEQUES PAYABLE TO HORSEMAN BROS
PROPRIETORS — G. F. HORSEMAN
J. E. HORSEMAN

PRIVATE CARS FOR HIRE.
STORAGE FOR 100 CARS.
30 LOCK-UP GARAGES.

Horsemans' Garage

OPEN
DAY & NIGHT
TELEPHONE:
WHITLEY BAY 275.

AUTOMOBILE
AND
ELECTRICAL
ENGINEERS.

OFFICIAL TECALEMIT STATION
HIGH PRESSURE GREASING & WASHING
WELDING & BRAZING
ACCUMULATORS CHARGED
LUCAS SPARES & BATTERIES

HEAD OFFICE:
MARINE GARDENS, WHITLEY BAY,
NORTHUMBERLAND.
ALSO AT MARINE AVENUE, WHITLEY BAY, NORTHUMBERLAND

CYLINDERS REBORED
BLACK & DECKER PROCESS FOR DECARBONIZING
CELLULOSE SPRAY PAINTING
CRANK SHAFT GRINDINGS

Mr. Koppem, 28, Thorntree Drive, Monkseaton.   August 1948.

DATE	Ford.8. ARA. 184.	LABOUR		MATERIAL
July. 19.	Remove petrol tank and repair.Gas and Material.	1.	1. 3	
24th.	Repairs and material.		7. 9.	
		£1	9 0.	

TEL. 275. .... 1/9/ 1948   2229
WITH
Received from 4. Koppen   THANKS
the sum of £ 1 : 9 0
Signature

HORSEMAN BROS.,
HEAD OFFICE:
MARINE GARDENS, WHITLEY BAY, NTHLD.,
Also at
MARINE AVENUE, WHITLEY BAY.

E. & O.E.   Ford

Horseman's Garage, on Marine Gardens, occupied a massive area and was open day and night.

Many attempts have been made by car enthusiasts to identify the make and model of the vehicle, but, alas, without success. It simply says on the back of the photograph 'Dennis, parked up on WB Links.'

Going shopping in Whitley Bay in a bygone era was a delight. The Library was a stationery shop situated on Whitley Road, around 1910. They also sold purses and trinkets.

Shepherd's newspaper, magazine and tobacco shop on Whitley Road in 1900. The owner, Mrs Shepherd, also cut people's hair in the shop. Not over the baccy, please!

Walter Kerr's stationery shop on Whitley Road sold birthday cards as well as writing paper and pens.

Giovanni Povesi's Assembly Rooms occupied the first floor of this building on Whitley Road around the year 1900. The accommodation included spacious and well-furnished rooms, smoke rooms, reading rooms and cuisine of the finest order.

Shopping in the 1980s, on the junction of Park Avenue and Whitley Road. From left to right is the Whitley Bay Organ Centre, continental butcher Van Der Lann, florist Rennison Rae, Mayfair Jewellers and Key Cutters and travel operator Lunn Polly. Upstairs is the Belvedaire Café.

Newsagent C. North & Son on Norham Road. With its old-fashioned white tile-effect bricks and wood surround, you can imagine this shop easily blending in with those found at Beamish Museum. Now long gone, the picture of the shop was taken in 1973.

William Pattinson's store, in Station Road, sold a comprehensive stock of glass, china, earthenware and art ware.

Stephen Fry's tea room called Panama House. Literally thousands of people flocked here over the summer months. It was immensely popular.

Panama House owner Stephen Fry erected his 'bungalow' (the local newspaper's term for Panama House) in the mid-1890s. One of the first men who understood publicity, he arranged for top bands and entertainment troupes to perform there, thus helping to bring in the crowds to his place for teas, dinners and suppers. Mr Fry was also dressed as he is in his picture, smartly attired in the best clothes, complete with a peaked hat and deck shoes.

The inhabitants of Percy Road in the 1890s were from middle-class backgrounds. Most held good jobs as doctors and solicitors. Because they were well paid, they could also afford the luxury of having maids and butlers. The properties in Percy Road were built in 1873 by a builder called Alfred Styan – not single-handedly of course!

A schoolboy has his picture taken in Gladstone Adams Photographic Studio in Station Road, Whitley Bay. Unlike today where easy digital photography is at hand, the only place to get your picture taken if you did not have a family camera was at a professional photographers.

This is a rare picture of John Welch (left), whose confectionery factory was situated on Laburnum Avenue, Whitley Bay. It's still there but no longer making sweets. Welch's produce was sent to many parts of the world, including Scandinavia. But there is another link to the factory: Denise Welch, more popularly known as a major actress on television and radio. Denise grew up in Tynemouth, but I expect she made several visits to the factory as a child – her very own Willy Wonka's! Another famous local was Cullercoats fishwife Polly Donkin, who coined the familiar catchphrase of Welch's toffee: 'It's just so lovely and doesn't stick to your teeth!'

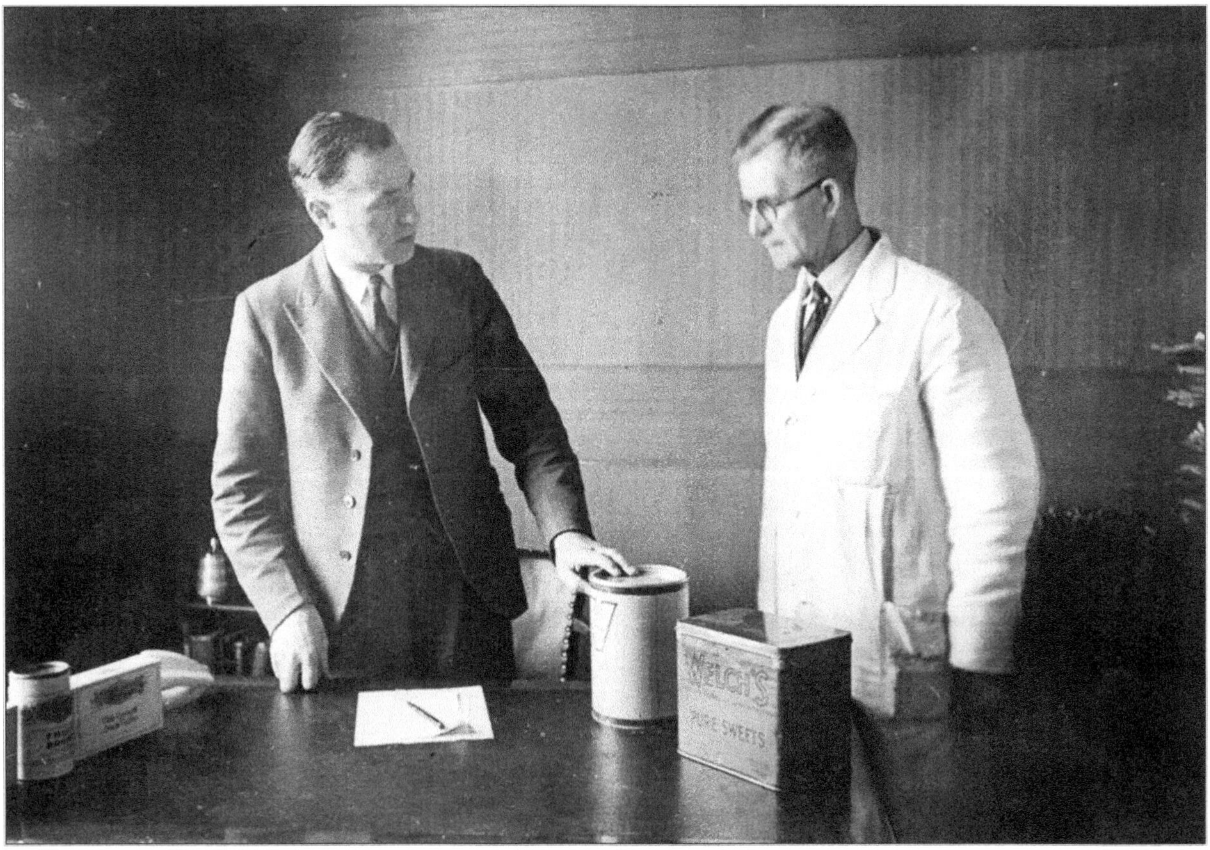

John Welch pictured in 1937. Items on the table include Cream Toffees, Assorted Fruit Selection and Fruit Drops. It'll be curious to know whether anyone has this packaging in their loft.

John W. Welch's factory in Laburnum Avenue, pictured here in 1936. A local resident recalls the aroma from the factory was very strong. 'I could smell it like it was next door and I lived two streets away!'

Mr W.J. Bullock's shop stood on Whitley Road, and is seen here in about 1910. A confectioner and fancy bread maker, Mr Bullock was exceedingly proud of his fine reputation. It had been built up over the years through selling bread made only from the 'best cereal ingredients'. The shop also sold jellies, ices, cordials, and other appetisers, all guaranteed to make the mouth water.

Gordon College in Gordon Square, under the guidance of principal Miss Rimington. In 1900 the classrooms were large and airy, and were built especially to accommodate a vast number of children per lesson. Reading from the pre-term literature, it says 'The teachers are pleasant but very strict and teach a complete syllabus, ranging from Maths and English, to foreign languages, with the aid of overseas visiting mistresses.'

If you needed a woolly hat on a winter's day, then you would not have far to go if you lived in Whitley Bay. Adamson's on Park View were at hand in the late 1960s.

Ale merchants Aitchie's certainly knew how to brew a good pint. As seen from this advert from 1937, you could buy your Aitchie's ale locally and sing a song or two. How about warbling their theme tune 'Oh Aitchie's ales, I love you'!

Good old Mary Russell, making her rugs! Wool specialist Mary came from a bygone era where people actually made mats, rather them buying them two for £1 at a cut-price store. As outlined in the advert, this is a 'craft which is followed by filmstars – and even SAILORS!'

Mr T. Thompson was a house furnisher and upholsterer who had premises on Station Road, Whitley Bay and in Newcastle upon Tyne. In the past proprietors preferred to have their names above their shops, instead of opting for the sort of catchy names we see on the high streets today. Mr Thompson also sold a selection of carpets, floorcloths and linoleums.

Older shoppers will recall the Co-op in Whitley Bay having an upstairs department, where it sold clothes. This advert from the *Seaside Chronicle* endeavours to entice shoppers in for Christmas bargains. So what would the man in the new year of 1967 be wearing? How about a 'society' (meaning 'posh') dressing gown in the mornings. Or maybe socks and handkerchiefs?

CHAPTER FIVE

The Town Today

Itook all the photographs in this chapter, the majority of which were snapped over the last few months of 2006 and the early part of 2007. In that short time, the magic shop in Park View has been replaced by a hair extensions outlet, and the regeneration of Whitley Bay's Spanish City and the surrounding area has been given the go-ahead by the local council. As you look at the pictures contained within this chapter, wonder what will change over the coming years – or indeed months! If it makes you get you digital camera out, then I have achieved what I have set out to achieve. More people taking more pictures and capturing living history.

Whitley Road, in 2005, on the traffic light crossing, with the Ship to the left. While the shopping mall does well, the smaller shops have taken it hard. Whitley Road coming from the Station Hotel upward has seen many shop closures, and the Co-op and other food stores are also feeling the pinch.

Eastbourne Gardens in 2004. The post office closed down due to government policies, as pensions and benefits switched to banks and holes in the wall. In 2007 the old post office in Whitley Bay is now an estate agent.

Park View in 2005. Two pedestrians and a dog look puzzled as to why the council suddenly put this tall black pole in the middle of the pavement. It transpired some weeks later that it was to attach a traffic sign, similar to the one visible in the picture.

St Paul's Church grounds in the summer of 2006. Over the years changes have been made to the placings of the tomb stones in order to accommodate building an extension. This caused annoyance to some Whitley Bay residents, whose late family members were buried in the plots.

It is a sorry fact that this chapter will hold memories for people in the future. It is dubious as to whether this old outside seating area in the vicinity of the tennis courts and Victoria Avenue will still be around in 10 years time.

A cold, frosty day on Norham Road, Whitley Bay, in 2002. It's often confused with Norham Road, North Shields, but only by the post office workers!

In January 2007 the gentleman who runs this post office in Front Street, Monkseaton, was unable to give a 'yes' or 'no' answer as to whether it would survive the Labour government's downscaling plans of the post offices in the UK. In other words, its closure. But it's not only a case of where to buy a stamp: the post office is a community meeting place, mainly for the elderly. It's a shame so many have closed. Perhaps the post office will be entirely phased out, in which case this will be a rare photograph in 50 years.

Monkseaton is renowned for hardly changing its look down this lower half of Front Street. An opticians currently occupies this prized spot across the road.

Broken television sets and video cassette recorders stand stacked, waiting to be collected in this rather 'sign of the times' photograph. A piece of graphitti seems to put the finishing touches to this eyesore.

As satellite TV grew in popularity, bigger and more powerful dishes were attached to walls and became ugly, especially in residential areas. This picture shows two massive dishes on the back of a house in Queen's Road and would not be allowed today. A council restriction exists on one dish and its size.

This would be a fine place to live in Norham Road, Whitley Bay. However, it is not a dwelling but the headquarters for British Telecom (BT).

Formerly Charlie Brown's Garage on Marden Road, Whitley Bay, this building escaped demotion and instead was refurbished to house a sports centre with a watery feel. It opened in early 2007.

It's no joke that this magic shop on Park View did not last long. Just over a year to be precise. Indeed, it lived up to its name and swiftly disappeared and was replaced by a hair extension hairdressers.

The YMCA in Whitley Bay closed its doors for good in 2006. It was boarded up and was about to be demolished as this book went to press. Rock star Sting is known to have gone there as a child.

The same YMCA building, showing signs of graffitti. This was the original, grand main entrance.

Above on Marden Bridge, the fine structure of the building in all its glory.

This is Poppyknots sandwich and soft drinks shop on Park View. It was in business for just over two years before finally closing its doors.

Probably one of the best newsagents in Whitley Bay, still going strong with a brilliant service record. In January 2007 Bruce Robinson was the owner in Park View, Whitley Bay. He was also known to deliver the newspapers when the paper boys phoned in sick. Good man!

Nicholson the butcher is another stalwart. Top service and a long line of regular customers. Can't be bad. Their shop, also in Park View, has a homely exterior.

Whitley Bay Boy's Club Under-13s – pictured here on 18 September 2004, in Park View Shopping Centre on the day of its official opening.

Looking out to Whitley Road in January 2007, from the area of the council offices.

Two people outside outside the Co-op building on a summer day in July on Marden Road in 2004.

Marden Bridge School in 2007. Formerly a grammar school, it switched to state school status in the early 1970s. Its vast field allowed recreation building extensions to be built on its grounds.

The former Allesta Ballroom in Esplanade, Whitley Bay, in October 2006 looks in a sorry state. But then again, what's new?

The Monseaton Arms in December 2006 – the satellite dishes the only giveaway that it is the 21st century!

The peace and tranquillity of The Crescent in Whitley Bay in 2002. The railway line is to the right.

An almost festive Christmas card view of St Paul's Church in December 2005, with the council lights on the trees only just visible.

The steps leading up on to Marden Bridge, Whitley Bay, in 1996. As an 11-year-old in 1973, I remember climbing these on my way to Marden Bridge Middle School. While I am now 45 years old, the steps have not aged a bit!

The High Point on the seafront in 2007. This place was a hive of activity for many years, with parties, wedding receptions and birthday bashes being held here, plus singers. It has fallen into disrepair and now stands in a sorry state.

Whitley Road, January 2006. As we have learned from this book, no building is totally sacred from the bulldozers. It may be the case within 20 years time that this area may be flattened to make way for development.

John W. Welch's sweet factory had long gone out of business when this photograph was taken in June 2006, yet it is still there, almost spookily bearing the sign of business above the door.

Whitley Bay Police Station. At the time of the compilation of this book, plans were afoot to move the station lower down to where the library is, near the one-way system, on Park Avenue.

The Whitley Bay Cenotaph, still standing proud in memory of the lives of all those lost in wars, whether they be in uniform or civilians. More appropriate because of the loss of life in the Middle East and beyond.

What can you say about The Bedroom pub? By 2007 it stood for nothing more than a loud drinking den and would-be nightclub – like its next door neighbour The Fire Station bar. What does it say about society when a bar opens to serve alcohol at 9am? Much to the displeasure of local residents, the Fire Station won the right to serve early in the morning – however, it is just an 11am start for The Bedroom.

The Whitley Bay Council Office on the corner of Victoria Mews, Whitley Bay, in 2007. This building was refurbished in 2006 at the cost of thousands to residents. And in keeping with usual council thinking, just 12 months later it was decided to move the council offices to again!

If you take the car and tarmac away from this view of Park Avenue, with the church in view it could be 100 years ago. Such a church scene is timeless.

Whitley Bay seafront on a cold day in September 2005. The people in the photograph were actually tourists from Japan, and found it amusing that no other holidaymakers were there too!

The Berkley Tavern, still in business and as active as ever – a top Whitley Bay watering hole if ever there was one.

Park Avenue, leading down to the seafront, March 2005. This one-way system has been active for many years, with the road narrowed to cut down on speeding cars.

In January 2007 you would find this community building facing the Whitley Bay Library.

There might be life in the old dog yet. Currently, The Avenue pub is boarded up and may unfortunately find its way on the demolition list. But it would be a sad day if Whitley Bay were to lose this once-prized hotel, considering its age and history.

A full view of The Avenue. Its full size is apparent but whether the structure is sound is another matter.

This is one side of the old Porthole Pub which faced Whitley Bay seafront. It has stood empty for years and finally looks set for the chop.

In January 2007, Whitley Bay's council issued a new leaflet outlining its plans for the Spanish City. A proposal included a £5.5 million redevelopment of the Playhouse, renovation of the Spanish City Dome, millions invested into a new swimming pool, improving The Links and redeveloping Whitley Park.

This barren land at the bottom of The Avenue is where the council offices and Priory Theatre once stood. Now just grass and soil, it is earmarked for the multi-million pound redevelopment.

Looking up Marine Avenue, towards the Berkley Tavern pub, from a coastal direction in November 2007. There are plans afoot to fill the gaps and for a bit more knocking down.

This little wishing well located just off The Links is not actually a well. It's two feet deep! But you may have guessed that already. Few people look into it to check.

The Whitley Bay Library won't be around long as soon as the new development gets underway. But no fear, it is not the end of the library, for it will be relocated and made larger.

If you go to Chapter Two of this book, you will see what a hive of activity the back of the Spanish City was. Droves of people packed into this area. By the early 1970s the fun park included The Ghost Train and other rides in the open air.

Barren land opposite Marine Park First School in February 2007, just waiting to be built on.

Marine Park First School replaced Coquet School. It is modern and gives the children a better education, although some former pupils of Coquet cried a tear or two over its passing, for it had educated residents' children for a century.

Looking up Marine Avenue, this amusements arcade looks destined to be demolished.

The Rainbow Amusements, still hanging in there. But empty and looking bleak. Its future, too, is in the balance.

Whitley Bay Playhouse in December 2006. A council proposal included a major redevelopment of the theatre, which includes a much larger seating area and eating and drinking facilities.

This wonderful church has so far managed to avoid the bulldozer. But with so many churches being pulled down and smashed to pieces, its future is very much in doubt.

This corner shop in Eastbourne Gardens started its decline in the mid-1980s. It was sold on to a buyer who tried to make a go of it, but it appears it is in the wrong place, especially when there is another corner shop further up doing good trade.

Norham Road in Whitley Bay on a very cold winter's day. The property just out of camera shot, with the white door, to the far right used to be Colin Leith's TV and Video Repair Shop. It closed due to fallen trade and the owner converted the property into flats.

Infracombe Gardens in 2004, looking up to Whitley Road, the van turning the corner where the traffic lights are.

Rockcliffe Bowling Club still attracts all ages to its grounds. It is one of the few outdoor local activities available for older people.

The success of the large supermarkets have not sent Spar out of business. In fact, Spar is hugely popular with Monkseaton customers who 'want to be in and out with no long queues'. And who can blame them!

A National Heritage protected house, solid and built to last more than 100 years ago, on Front Street, Monkseaton, in 2007, it has hardly altered.

Looking over the bridge of Monkseaton Metro Station railway lines, in the direction of Longbenton. Although these lines are repaired and maintained, they are very durable. Part of the goods entrance on the right was converted into a childcare facility.

A lovely pictorial scene of the beach and incoming tide in Whitley Bay in June 2004. The café on the left has exchanged hands over the years but remains a nice quiet place to grab a cup of tea or coffee and a slice of cake, and relax while looking out to the beach and sea.

This corner shop at the bottom of Percy Road used to be called Brown's, a simple newspaper seller and off licence. But Mr Brown died some time ago. It's now called Quix, selling food as well as newspapers, drinks and sweets.

The holidaymakers might not come to Whitley Bay in their droves like they used to do, but you cannot change nature and this beautiful sight of the beach and shore, in 2007.

By 2007 property became a valuable asset. It seems curious that this splendid old house was boarded up on Victoria Avenue, a popular place to live at the time.

June 2006. One of the crumbling buildings in Whitley Road. Some of the arch segments have fallen out, causing the upper bit to be unsafe. You can actually see where the stone has come loose, to the upper left of the picture.

The closure of Whitley Fabrics on Norham Road in February 2007, with a simple whitewash notice saying 'we are moving'. They had already moved!

Souter Park, Monkseaton, in 2006. The bowling green is still very popular during the spring and summer months.

The renovation of a splendid old house on Sanderson Road, Whitley Bay, in 2007. This area is full of traditional dwellings like this one, very large and spacious. Some of the properties around here almost border on the million-pound mark.

Marine Avenue retains the respectability of its past. It is a well-built street full of very big houses with large gardens. Indeed, the gardens are so extensive that a property owner in a nearby street received permission to build a new five-bedroom house in his back garden! These are some of the most expensive properties in Whitley Bay.

Marine Avenue Medical Centre is a new building on Marine Avenue, to take the place of an older property further down the road which has been sold and converted back to a dwelling.

The Tennis Courts just off Marine Avenue, another recreation area which pulls in sports-minded people. This hut has stood here for decades. However, it is in need of some maintenance judging from this picture taken in January 2007.

Looking a bit worse for wear, February 2007. Large billboards used to occupy this spot on the corner on Norham Road. They were taken down and the rubbish behind from a sandwich shop on Park View was all there to see.

St Paul's Church Hall on King's Drive in 2007. It was converted to house a business making audio book tapes for the blind.

Looking from King's Drive to the junction of Queen's Road in 2007. Most of the cars you see here don't belong to the residents but office workers.

The Indian Oceon Tandoori Restaurant at the bottom on Marine Avenue, Whitley Bay, in October 2006.

The Porthole from the front: boarded up, bricked up, set alight and vandalised. It seems it has had the full works and looks beyond repair. It might need to be pulled down before it falls down.

BV - #0120 - 280426 - C0 - 265/195/14 - PB - 9781780914459 - Gloss Lamination